AIR TRAFFIC
CONTROL AND MANAGEMENT

AIR TRAFFIC
CONTROL AND MANAGEMENT

BY

WILLIAM BROWN
BAYLEN FLETCHER

KNOWLEDGE BAKERS

ISBN: 9789390013227 (HB)

Published by : **Knowledge Bakers**
Pune, India
Email: knowledgebakers2019@gmail.com

Digitally Printed at : **Replika Press Pvt. Ltd.**

PREFACE

Air Traffic Control (ATC) and Management are vital components of the aviation industry, responsible for the safe and efficient movement of aircraft in the airspace. The processes involved in air traffic control and management are complex and involve several stakeholders, including air traffic controllers, pilots, airlines, and air navigation service providers. We will explore the key concepts of air traffic control and management, its importance in the aviation industry, and how it has evolved over time. One of the essential aspects of air traffic control and management is the use of advanced technologies. The aviation industry relies on sophisticated technologies to ensure the safe and efficient operation of aircraft. Radar, satellite navigation, and communication systems are just a few examples of the technologies used in air traffic control and management. These technologies enable air traffic controllers to monitor and manage the movement of aircraft in the airspace, providing real-time information on aircraft position, altitude, speed, and direction. Another critical aspect of traffic control and management is airspace management. Airspace is divided into several sectors, each of which is managed by air traffic controllers. Air traffic controllers are responsible for ensuring that each sector's capacity is not exceeded, and the flow of air traffic is optimized to prevent congestion and delays. Air traffic controllers must also coordinate with other controllers in adjacent sectors to ensure a smooth transition of aircraft between sectors.

Safety is paramount in the aviation industry, and air traffic control and management play a critical role in ensuring it. Air traffic controllers are responsible for maintaining safe separation between aircraft in the airspace. They must ensure that aircraft maintain a safe distance from each other to prevent collisions. Air traffic controllers must also monitor weather conditions and communicate any hazards to pilots to ensure safe flight operations. The aviation industry has evolved significantly over the years, and air traffic control and management have played a critical role in its growth. The introduction of new technologies, such as satellite navigation, has enabled air traffic controllers to monitor and manage aircraft more efficiently. The development of new aircraft and the expansion of the aviation industry have also necessitated improvements in air traffic control and management. The aviation industry has evolved significantly over the years, and air traffic control and management have played a significant role in its growth. The tragic events of 9/11 highlighted the importance of air traffic control and management in ensuring aviation safety, leading to significant improvements in aviation security measures.

This book covers various topics related to air traffic management and control, including the history, regulations, and stakeholders involved in the aviation industry. It explores the importance of occupational health and safety in air traffic management and how it affects the performance and efficiency of air traffic controllers. It also covers the basics of deep learning networks and their applications in air traffic management. It discusses the use of behavioural modelling paradigms in designing power electronic converters for more electric aircraft and the basics of power electronics and their applications in aviation. It could be helpful for aviation management and regulatory bodies to understand the current state and future trends of air traffic management and could be a valuable resource for students and academics studying aviation or related fields, including engineering, computer science, and management.

We are grateful to all those persons as well as various books, manuals, periodicals, magazines, journals etc. that helped in the preparation of this book. In spite of the best efforts, it is possible that some errors may have occurred into the compilation and editing of the book. Further queries, constructive suggestions and criticisms for the improvement of the book are always welcomed and shall be thankfully acknowledged.

William Brown
Baylen Fletcher

CONTENTS

SECTION-III

HUMAN FACTOR

Section 1

Introduction

Chapter 1

Introductory Chapter: Management and Control of Air Traffic

1. Introduction

After the World War I, a large number of aircraft serving the war turned to civil use. France and Britain successively established airlines, forming an aviation network connecting countries centered on Europe. During the World War II, aviation technology developed rapidly, which laid a solid foundation for the development of civil aviation after the war. B707 is the first generation of jet airliner. Since then, many second-generation jet airliners have appeared in the 1960s, with representative models of B727 and IL 62. In the 1970s, the third-generation jetliner with wide fuselage represented by B747 appeared. The "Concorde" supersonic aircraft jointly developed by Britain and France was officially put into operation on January 21, 1976. However, due to many factors such as high fuel consumption, short range, serious noise pollution, and high operating cost, the "Concorde" aircraft announced its retirement in October 2003. In recent decades, with the rapid development of civil aircraft, its safety, economy, and comfort have been greatly improved. All this comes from the extensive use of composite structures and the upgrading of airborne equipment.

A modern air transportation system can provide very strong service capacity to meet the different needs of various potential users [1, 2]. To meet the different needs of different users for services, the modern air transport system uses advanced technology, equipment, facilities, operation rules, and procedures, and is managed by well-trained, skilled, and well-educated people. Compared with other transportation modes such as highway, railway and sea transportation, air transportation system is a system with high efficiency, high cost, and very sensitive to the changes of internal and external factors.

2. Characteristics of air traffic management and control

Air traffic management is a safe, economic, efficient, dynamic, and comprehensive management of air traffic and airspace. The first-generation of air traffic management is characterized by land-based air traffic control equipment, including land-based communication, navigation, and monitoring equipment. The second-generation air traffic management integrates satellite communication, navigation, and monitoring technologies, improves the processing and transmission of information, expands the scope of monitoring, and improves the navigation accuracy through the global navigation satellite system, to reduce the spacing between aircraft and increase the capacity of airspace. The future navigation system is a complex global system, which is related to many business categories and interests, such as national defense, homeland security, air traffic, commercial and general aviation, commercial aerospace transportation, passenger and cargo transportation, military flight, and airport. The types of aircraft operating in the future environment will not only increase, but also the performance envelope will become wider, and it is also required to operate in the same airspace, which increases the complexity of air traffic management. The sustainable development and growth of aviation require environmental protection and reduce the adverse impact of noise and emissions on air quality. Even with the increase of air traffic, it will be significantly reduced compared with today. At the same time, it is also necessary to mitigate the impact of aviation on water quality, energy use, and climate.

3. Summary and conclusion

As air traffic grows, so does the need for efficient, globally harmonized and interoperable Air Traffic Management (ATM). A structured and globally harmonized ATM framework, supported by a cost-effective and sustainable Communications, Navigation and Surveillance (CNS) infrastructure, should be developed in the future.

References

[1] ICAO Doc 9854 AN/458. Global Air Traffic Management Operation Concept. 1st ed. Montreal, Canada: ICAO; 2005

[2] ICAO Doc 9750 AN/963. Global Air Navigation Plan. 3rd ed. Montreal, Canada: ICAO; 2007

Section 2

Air Traffic Control

Chapter 2

Key Aspects of Occupational Health and Safety towards Efficiency and Performance in Air Traffic Management

Abstract

This paper/chapter deals with the key drivers for adopting and developing an Occupational Health and Safety System (OHS) with a special focus on air traffic management and traffic controller's workplace. A such system includes regulation and legal compliance procedures, actions and monitoring for ensuring workplace safety, incentives and motivation for the air traffic controller and associate personnel health and wellbeing. By a systemic approach, the key characteristics of OHS towards air traffic management are presented, highlighting the key aspects for implementing a quality management system in air traffic control, which is the cornerstone of airport operation efficiency and productivity on one hand; and the nature of job and the intensive working environment is well recognised. Based on air traffic providers functional analysis the key occupational aspects for air traffic control are taken into consideration, providing the benefits for implementing quality management systems (QMS) and OHS is real business. Conventional wisdom is to highlight the importance for establishing and incorporating a modern custom-made OHS system in accordance with the requirements addressed by OHSAS 18001 to develop and implement a QMS for air traffic services. Contribution of this paper is to highlight the key priorities for managers and decision makers in field of air traffic services providers, depicting ways and recommendation for adopting an efficient path for implementing OHS in a QMS environment.

Keywords: occupational health and safety, air traffic management, quality management, performance management

1. Introduction

In general, Occupational Health and Safety (OHS) deals with the provision of safe and secure working conditions for all employees of a company or business units. Institutionally, occupational safety refers to the comprehensive safety efforts, plans, and implementations throughout the entire organization, considering health and safety risks for the employees driven by both sides the inside working and the outside business environment. Especially for the air traffic providers, due to the complexity and multitasking air traffic controlling procedures, the dedicated infrastructures, and high use of electronic equipment, as well as their communication interrelationship with different functions of airport business, the need for evaluation, review, and secure OHS is essential.

The investment in personnel expertise, skills, and abilities are essential for air traffic providers, considering the special skills and abilities are required for delivering air traffic control services. Therefore, for air traffic providers, even in units/airports that the volume of traffic controllers is not large, there is a tendency for shifting from personal OHS responsibility delivered by managers to a more horizontal and institutional action providing harmonization achieved by institutional safety framework promoting innovation and standardization across this business sector. This clearly demonstrates the significance of complete OHS, where the term "total" denotes that safety issues must be considered at all levels of the organization and in all operations, without dismissing or eliminating any organizational, production, or service-related issues.

The commitment of public and private organizations to improve their competitiveness through service or product quality has resulted in the need for a new management system that considers their operations. Moreover, different approaches are required due to the diversity of production processes and business sectors. The increase in these requirements has highlighted the importance of a systematic approach to dealing with them. In numerous cases, the practice has shown that modern management standards for the development of relevant management systems can provide efficient and effective operation and a working environment while also having the inherent ability to support continuous quality improvement [1].

When an organization has a quality management system (QMS) in place, it can provide the proper context for a systematic approach to standardizing aspects such as quality, environmental protection, occupational health and safety, social responsibility, and possibly many others. A QMS frequently shares various stakeholders, resources, and processes; thus, system integration is critical for organizations to save time, effort, cost, and resources [2].

The drivers for implementing an appropriate Occupational Health and Safety (OHS) System within the operational framework of an existing QMS can be classified as regulatory, financial, marketing, operational, and social. The most important motivations for them include complying with the legal framework, ensuring workplace safety, personnel health and motivation, responding to government appeals, and remaining competitive or gaining a competitive advantage [3].

It is noteworthy that the International Civil Aviation Organization (ICAO) guidelines and obligations, as well as other aviation institutions' recommendations and regulations, highlight a continuing trend of air transport growth in Europe in many reports. Air Navigation Services Providers' (ANSPs') operational and administrative efficiency and effectiveness are critical to the quality of air traffic management (ATM). The Occupational Health and Safety (OHS) of ANSPs operational workplace is one of the main parameters that support the quality of services and plays an important role in the new era of air transport development and sustainable aviation growth.

The OHS management system is at the top of the agenda in relevant national and international discussions, particularly in countries where aviation growth is directly related to productivity, the attractiveness and competitiveness of the business environment, and economic stability. This paper deals with the framework and the characteristics of the two management systems (QMS and OHS). It is presented the needs and the challenges to improve OHS in the management systems of ANSPs, by implementing a modern OHS system based on relevant international standards and best practices. By a systemic analysis, the characteristics of QMS and OHS are given, providing the benefits towards integration and highlighting the main objective to develop an OHS system adapted to the operational characteristics and the quality management system of the Hellenic Air Navigation Services Provider (HANSP).

2. Quality management system objectives and outputs

2.1 Definitions and key principles

Quality management system (QMS) is a collection of all the actions are concerned with the quality decisions of an enterprise or business unit. It is a procedural manual associate with tools and applications that impact the development and delivery processes, services, and products. Therefore, QMS could be defined as "the manual" that clarify responsibilities in the organizational chart but also inside each business unit, illustrate the production procedures and services processes, and present the necessary resources to implement and deliver and all those to connected and represented with the quantitative and qualitative outputs and business objectives of an enterprise/unit business or action plan.

Effective implementation of a QMS is to be an essential component of management and production. A well-executed QMS will not make an organization more profitable, efficient, or customer-focused in and of itself, but it will provide an organization with the inherent ability to improve its operations from production to sales. Particularly for businesses that operate and manage assets, infrastructures, and networks, where competition and business performance are concerned with customer satisfaction and operational efficiency [4, 5].

Furthermore, QMS is a significant contributor to authorities, organizations, enterprises, and business units focusing on their objectives and goals on the one hand and ensuring that production activity output provides a higher level of service to customers, minimizes waste time, provides necessary resources to employees, and follows a continuous improvement approach to all actions and deliverables on the other. The following are the key drivers of a modern QMS in accordance with the International Organization for Standardization (ISO) requirements (as determined by a review of the ISO 9000 series) [3]:

- Clear, coherent, and positive commitment towards management quality and decision-making process;
- Bidirectional action between top management and all levels or group of employees promoting a corporate stigma representing the working environment culture and initiatives, linked with the personal performance, skills, and improvements;
- Implementation of a performance and procedural monitoring system, supporting decisions and depicting the internal working environment including employees behavioral over actions and miscommunication (a critical issue especially for the air traffic controllers);
- Introduce and maintain Human Resources (HR) procedures meeting the needs of each job/task, promoting innovation and support training to meet occupational and personal needs for all employees.

2.2 QSM benefits

Literature supporting the key benefits of a QMS is growing, promoting the need for adopting OHS to achieve performance in air traffic providers. In other words, research in the aviation sector recognized that air traffic controllers OHS conditions and aviation business performance are strongly linked. The direct benefits in aviation business operation could be summarized in the following's issues [3]:

- Customer satisfaction;
- Quality of service;
- Employee satisfaction and commitment to the management targets and goals;
- Operational management and a more effective workforce operation;
- Improved supplier relations; and
- Improved corporate stigma and brand.

In the aviation sector, all the above are crucial also in terms of traffic demand and destination marketing, as airports are the gates of a region to the international market, and the level of service promotes the image of a city or a region or an industry [6].

In terms of management performance, there are also essential opportunities towards:

- Achievement of corporate goals and assess the cost and benefits to meet those goals;
- Reduce bureaucracy, misunderstandings and promote fairness in responsibilities allocation and task delivery;
- Clarify responsibilities and expectations, promoting bonus schemes towards efficiency and productivity;
- Clarify mechanisms for multi-objective and multitasking decisions promoting cooperation, team working and effective communication;
- Award and recognize the performance of the employee and involve them in the review and improvement of their work.

ISO 9000 is a set of quality management and quality assurance standards designed to assist all types of business structures, promoting the QMS key elements in broad use as it is not industry-specified, providing flexibility to be applied. The ISO 9000 group of protocols includes the following standards [7–9]:

- ISO 9000: 2015: quality management systems—fundamentals and vocabulary (definitions).
- ISO 9001: 2015: quality management systems—requirements.
- ISO 9004: 2009: quality management systems—managing for the sustained success of an organization (continuous improvement).
- ISO 19011: 2011: guidelines for auditing quality management systems.

The ISO 9000: 2015 and ISO 9001: 2015 standards are based on the seven quality management principles listed below, which senior management can use to improve their organizations. The field of QMS is concerned with [9]:

- Customer satisfaction
- Leadership
- Engagement of people
- Process management
- Performance improvement
- Evidence-based decision making
- Relationship management

ISO 9000 is a process-oriented approach to documenting and reviewing the structure, responsibilities, and procedures required to achieve effective quality management in an organization. It is based on the Plan-Do-Check-Act (PDCA) methodology. Organizations find that using ISO 9001 helps them because it specifies the requirements for an effective quality management system [8, 9]:

- Organize a QMS.
- Create satisfied customers, management, and employees.
- Continually improve.

2.3 QMS implementation and certification

Professionals involved in the development, implementation, auditing, and management of an ISO quality management system, as well as quality professionals interested in updating their documented ISO 9001-based QMS, can enroll in ISO 9000 training courses, which include ISO 9001 and quality management system courses. Furthermore, organizations seeking to improve employee performance and employees seeking to continuously improve will find ISO 9000 training useful [9].

The QMS recommended in ISO 9001: 2015 quality management systems—requirements is still process-based, its focal point is management leadership, which is linked by feedback loops to the enterprise's planning, support, and operational activities, as well as results assessment and improvement. The PDCA cycle (Plan-Do-Check-Act) underpins the entire quality management system concept. Building a management system in accordance with the new ISO 9001: 2015 guidelines requires an organization to analyze its context based on knowledge and understanding of its operational essence in relation to its immediate and distant environment. This aids in the efficient management of the created system, allowing the strategic business objectives to be met [9, 10].

Certification in accordance with the ISO 9001 standard can boost an organization's credibility by demonstrating to customers that its products and services meet both standards and expectations. In some cases, certification is required or mandated by law. The certification process entails implementing ISO 9001: 2015 requirements and then successfully completing a registrar's audit confirming the organization meets those requirements. Training can provide an opportunity to review the ISO 9001: 2015 standard as well as apply quality management principles in a practical setting [9].

3. Occupational health and safety system (OHS)

3.1 Objectives and outputs

OHS is a term that refers to providing a safe and secure working environment for all organization's employees. Employee safety concerns are becoming increasingly important, not only in the workplace but in all aspects of our societies' activities and it's the cornerstone for corporate social responsibility plan for most of the high "branded" enterprises. Theoretically, there are two directions for managing safety: (a) institutional safety and (b) individual safety. Institutional safety refers to the total safety efforts and implementations throughout the entire organization, taking into account both the inside and outside environments [11].

Due to the complexity of processes, infrastructures, and equipment, as well as their interrelationship between different sectors of the organization, there is now a profound need for safety to be expanded from individual to institutional safety. This clearly demonstrates the significance of total OHS, where the term "total" means that safety issues must be considered at all levels of the organization and in all activities, without disregarding or excluding any organizational, production, or service-related issues [12].

OHS has several inherent characteristics for providing a safe environment, the most important of which are [13]:

- Management commitment;
- Employee involvement;
- Hazard identification and control;
- Training, including soft skills training programs for abilities in communication and personal development;
- Education; and
- Risk management assessment and continuous improvement process all of the above.

Aside from those, there is a slew of other factors to consider for efficient and effective OHS management. They include, among other things, worksite cleanliness, emergency preparedness, contingency planning, employee OHS training procedures, and so on. OHS must be regarded as an integral part of work-system design, development, and training. Especially, the issue of training should be analyzed in terms of training hours per employee but also regarding the content of training, where the development of personal soft skill is in high priority [12, 13].

OHS processes are just as important as the rest of the manufacturing and operational processes (design, production, manufacturing and marketing, etc.). Improving manufacturing processes without also improving working conditions will not result in a productive and safe manufacturing environment [11].

Employee involvement is a critical component of OHS implementations. A number of formal approaches, similar to process improvement, have been developed to encourage employee participation. The majority of these approaches are also important sources of data for quality improvement [13].

OHS is primarily concerned with reducing employee errors that may be caused by the environment and working conditions. OHS, through behavior-based safety management programs, does not treat accidents as performance errors but rather attempts to identify the fundamental causes of the errors. Employees are not permitted to use defective equipment or inappropriate methods. It may be possible to create more realistic tasking into account that daydreaming and boredom on the job frequently result in incidents or even more accidents caused by malfunctions in the perception system or distraction by others. In relation to the foregoing, OHS may [13]:

- Reduce insufficient equipment;
- Empower employees to be responsible for their equipment;
- Establish an ergonomic approach to workplace design;
- Reduce insufficient procedures;
- Establish an ergonomic work environment; and
- Reduce workplace risks, incidents, or accidents.

The issue of hazard prevention and accident control measures is essential crucial towards efficiency and successful OHS implementation. The analysis should be based on historical real data, and it should be based on comprehensive job safety or job hazard analyses over the business risks and the values at risk in the corporate environment [12, 13].

3.2 OHSAS 18001

OHS represents conditions and factors that already affect or could affect the health and safety of employees, other workers, visitors, or any other person in the workplace in any type of organization. Early in the 20th century, for the first time, standards and guidelines for OHS management were developed [14].

Moreover, ISO hosted a discussion in 1996, inviting many nations to develop international OHS Management Systems. The discussion included representatives from six international organizations, including ISO and the International Labor Organization (ILO), as well as governments, labor unions, employers, worldwide safety and health administrations, and insurance institutes. The Occupational Health and Safety Assessment Series—OHSAS 18000 was published in 1999 by the US Occupational Health and Safety Administration in collaboration with international certifying bodies from 15 countries across three continents. This set of standards is divided into two parts: OHSAS 18001 and OHSAS 18002. Several documents and standards were used in the development of these standards, including BS 8800: 1996, Technical Report NPR 5001:1997, Draft LRQA SMS 8800, and so on [14, 15].

Over the years, OHSAS 18001 has gained widespread acceptance, with firms of all sizes and industries implementing and certifying it. The standard has been updated, and the most recent version is BS OHSAS 18001: 2007 "Occupational Health and Safety Management Systems." Some countries refused to accept OHSAS 18001 and instead developed their own standards, which were mostly modifications of the International Labor Organization's "Guidelines on Occupational Safety and Health Management Systems" [15].

According to [15], the Occupational Health and Safety Assessment Series (OHSAS) Standard, as well as the accompanying OHSAS 18002, Guidelines for the Implementation of OHSAS 18001, were created in response to customer demand for a recognizable occupational health and safety management system standard against which their management systems could be assessed and certified. OHSAS 18001 was created to be compatible with the ISO 9001: 2000 (quality management) and ISO 14001: 2004 (environmental management) management system standards, allowing organizations to integrate quality, environmental, and occupational health and safety management systems if they so desire. In practice, the OHSAS Standard is reviewed and amended as needed.

The OHSAS Standard specifies the requirements for an OHS management system that allows an organization to develop and implement policies and objectives that take into account legal requirements and information about OHS risks. It is intended to apply to organizations of all sizes and types, as well as to accommodate a wide range of geographical, cultural, and social conditions [1, 4, 5, 16].

The system's success is dependent on commitment from all levels and functions of the organization, particularly top management. This type of system enables an organization to develop an OHS policy. The overall goal is to support and promote good OHS practices while keeping socioeconomic needs in mind. It should be noted that many of the requirements can be addressed at the same time or at a later date. The second edition of this OHSAS Standard focuses on clarifying the first edition and has taken into account the provisions of ISO 9001, ISO 14001, ILO-OSH, and other OHS management system standards or publications to improve compatibility for the benefit of the user community [15].

The OHSAS standard is based on the Plan-Do-Check-Act methodology (PDCA). PDCA can be summarized as follows [15]:

- Plan: define the objectives and processes required to achieve the desired results in accordance with the organization's OH&S policy;
- Do: put the processes in place;
- Check: monitor and measure processes in relation to OH&S policy, objectives, legal requirements, and other requirements, and report the results; and
- Act: take steps to improve OH&S performance on a continuous basis.

OHSAS 18001 is an international standard that specifies the requirements for an occupational health and safety framework. The key target is of this protocol deals with effective management of workplace risks and hazards to health and safety. It encompasses the organization's structure, planning activities, responsibilities, practices, directives, processes, and resources for designing, implementing, maintaining, and reviewing the organization's system and policy. For this system, everything is based on Deming's PDCA cycle for continuous improvement [13, 15].

The OHSAS 18001 standard underwent a significant revision in 2007, which resulted in the current structure and content of the standard is established. Many advantages can be gained from implementing this management system, including lower incident and accident rates, improved performance monitoring and accident reporting, better control of occupational health and safety risks, lower overall costs of accidents, lower insurance premiums, improved levels of compliance with health and safety legislation, reduced likelihood of fines and prosecutions, which may, in turn, result in less expensive insurance premiums, financial benefit, improved reputation, and long-term viability [13, 16].

According to the ILO and other organizations, 2.2 million workers die globally each year as a result of work-related accidents and diseases, 4 percent of the world's gross national product (GNP) is lost as a result of work-related accidents and diseases, and 6.300 workers die every day as a result of occupational accidents or work-related diseases. These statistics demonstrate that there is an urgent need for organizations all over the world to improve their health and safety management systems. Many consumers and customers expect businesses to be ethical in all aspects of their operations, including how they treat their employees [15, 16].

3.3 OAS accreditation

The implementation of OHS and certification in accordance with OHSAS 18001/ISO 45001 has a significant impact on operational performance. Certification has been shown to have significant benefits for the safety and economic components of abnormal operational performance, even for firms operating in environments with stringent safety regulations that already had above-average safety performance in comparison to their industry.

The practice has shown that as complexity and coupling increased, so did the benefits of certification. OHSAS certification resulted in significant increases in abnormal operational performance, with the greatest benefit accruing to firms with highly complex or coupled production systems. The relationship between safety certification, safety performance, and other operational performance outcomes was also clarified by operational evidence [15].

According to the institutional theory viewpoint, certification may be pursued primarily as a signaling device. The findings provided some support for this claim, with all of the significant increases in abnormal sales growth occurring after certification, despite the fact that the firms had above-average safety performance in their industries prior to certification.

However, the results revealed significant increases in abnormal performance in terms of safety, return on assets (ROA), sales growth, and productivity, indicating that certification provided more than just ceremonial benefits. The existence of increased abnormal safety and economic performance also sheds light on the ongoing debate over the relationship between safety and the economic components of operational performance [16].

OHSAS certification is unique in that firms seeking certification must replace existing OHSMS, so there is no reason to expect certification to improve operational performance. However, the findings are broadly consistent with previous research on other types of certification, implying that certified management systems that instill the processes and cognitions will improve operational performance in general.

4. QMS and OHS integration

4.1 Benefits and implementation challenges

Many businesses conduct QMS and OHS reviews or audits to evaluate their management performance. However, the outcomes of reviews and audits may not be a motivator for a sufficient and well-managed organization, owing to the fact that the majority of audits were contacted internally and focused on regulation and constitution compliance. As a result, performance-oriented messages to management are severely limited. A structured management system in which QMS and OHS are integrated within the organization, on the other hand, maybe more effective in promoting changes and reviewing performance [17].

It is worth noting that OHSAS Standards for OHS management are intended to improve business culture and benefit from the synergies of the combined management system. An organization may adopt its existing management system(s) to establish an OHS management system that meets the requirements of this OHSAS

Standard. However, it is noted that the application of various elements of the management system may differ depending on the intended purpose and the parties involved. The level of detail and complexity of the OHS management system, the extent of documentation, and the resources devoted to it are determined by a series of factors, including the system's scope, an organization's size and the nature of its activities, products, and services, and the organizational culture [15–18].

Integration of Management Systems (MS) could be partial or complete, as well as documental harmonization. The key issue is the degree of integration varies between two theoretical extremes [19]:

- The "zero" level, in which individual standardized MSs coexist in completely different ways; and
- Full integration, in which all elements and aspects of individual standardized MSs operate within one system.

These two extreme conditions are possible, but in practice, the level of integration will be somewhere in the middle. There is some evidence that QMS and OHS are successfully integrated, though OHSMS is perceived as less flexible, and there is less interest in integrating OHSMS with other systems [19].

There are two main methods for implementing and integrating MS. In the first, standards are implemented one at a time and then integrated. The other option is to implement multiple MSs at the same time and integrate them during the implementation process. When it comes to the two most popular management standards (QMS and EMS), the most common implementation and integration strategies are [19]:

- The QMS is implemented first and OHS second;
- The OHS is implemented first and QMS second and
- The QMS and OHS are implemented simultaneously.

The number of possible combinations grows as more systems (such as OHSAS 18001) are considered, but the implementation of the QMS first, followed by other systems, is most popular in organizations, according to the literature. QMS serves as a platform for integration for the vast majority of businesses. Companies are increasingly opting to implement ISO 9001, ISO 14001, and OHSAS 18001 all at the same time, combining them into a single management system (**Table 1**) [18, 19].

4.2 Implementation approach

OHS and QMS standards (ISO 9001:2015 and OHSAS 18001:2007) share a fundamental principle: continuous improvement based on Deming's cycle (Plan-Do-Check-Act). In the PDCA cycle, continuous improvement and incremental problem solving are represented. These four (4) steps can be used as a plan for the implementation of an effective and efficient integrated system based on certain stages of this management method (PDCA). The following are the specific steps [18, 19]:

1. The planning process is the first thing to do. This step entails making changes and improvements while also taking stock of the current situation and considering the potential outcomes. In real life, this means defining the problem, collecting relevant data, and determining the underlying cause of the problem.

Area	Target/output	Key components
Management system	Establishing, implement, maintain and continually improve the management systems (quality of service, environmental assessment, OHS and business risks) including the processes needed in accordance with the requirements of each International Standards	• The integration shared the same objective regards to policy, legal requirement and for continuous improvement for management system; • Integrated Management System (IMS) establish, implement and maintain a procedure(s) for dealing with actual and potential non-conformity for corrective and preventive action; • Formed the IMS appropriately, understood and applied within the organization for each management system
Corporate planning and strategy	Identification and evaluation of aspect, impacts and risks. Establish, implement and maintain the process to meet the requirement and determine the risk and opportunities that need to be addressed for each management system	• Identify an integrated risk control process covering service quality, environment, occupational health and safety aspects; • An integrated risk management system; • Establish, implement and maintain the management system policy that involved all the relevant units
Human resources (HR)	The relevant roles are assigned, communicated and understood whining the organization in term of requirement of International Standard	• Integrated reporting system for the performance of the QMS and OHS; • Benefits for proposals and actions lead to productive change or innovation
Integrated system operation	The integration formed the integrated monitoring and performance measurement in term of operational control for analysis and evaluation	• Effective integrated documentation and establish the document and record control; • Effective and continuing communication in the organization; • Integrated evaluation procedure in term of record, ensure the conformity of effectiveness for each system and applicable for legal requirements
Internal audit	The integration of the system leads the organization review about each management system as one system at the planned intervals, to ensure each continuing suitability, adequacy, and effectiveness	Establish the efficient and integrated audit in term of requirement for the management system, following the international standard and provide the information for the system to effectively implement the internal audit can be done in one time audit

Table 1.
Key components of the system integration.

2. The next step is to put the plan into action, which is known as executing. In this step, you must put into action the process you have already planned, using the information you gathered in the preceding step as a guide.

3. In order to control or implement an improvement, the third step is to check the process. This phase necessitated continual process monitoring and evaluation, as well as reporting on the results in relation to the objective and specification. At this point, we have completed the check phase and can draw conclusions about how effective implementation has been so far.

4. Acting, assessing effectiveness, as well as determining the function of implementation, are all part of the fourth step. The action that needs to be taken to further improve the result is in the act phase.

As it is obvious from the previous analysis:

- The first step (Plan) is to set a milestone for what the organization hopes to achieve, and the second step (Do) is required for implementation as management provides training, inspection by the committee, and review and completion of the security and environmental management system. Finally, the process is completed.

- A gap analysis, followed by a follow-up gap analysis, and fine-tuning of the management system are all steps in the third step (Check). This step also includes conducting an internal audit.

- In the last step (Act), the management will decide on future improvements in light of the external audit, and the management system certificate will be ready at the end of this phase.

5. Concluding remarks

The need to improve business competitiveness has driven quality, while government regulations and union pressure have increased security, while law and society have done their part to improve the environment. The management philosophy for these functions was retrospective, which was based on an analysis of indicators to show what had occurred. Statistical process control based on specifications that operators and equipment must meet has evolved into participative systems QMSs and total quality management from controlling at the end of the process to eliminate defective products.

QMS and OHS are two management areas that are part of an integrated system, which has a common structure and three branches. A highly integrated system of management structures should reflect the hierarchy established at all levels to develop, implement, and maintain each branch that affects a specific area of management in terms of organizational and responsibility allocation.

Increasing flexibility, efficiency, and competitiveness are three key benefits of integrating the OHS and QMS. There are a few factors in the integration that can provide management effectiveness and the main focus is on cost-effectiveness, management improvement, and system benefits [6, 20]. Any organization that uses a management system can use the proposed methodology. For this reason, the implementation efficiency can benefit greatly from the use of the PDCA methodology [21].

An integrated QMS system requires a specific tactic for implementation because, while standards for each of the aspects show some similarities, they do not show a common methodology for integrated system development. There has been a parallel development of both quality and safety based on management strategy and priorities, and this has a significant impact on the added value of enterprise management, which will be examined as part of the company's due diligence [21].

Acknowledgements

The paper use outputs developed in the research project "ENIRISST—Intelligent Research Infrastructure for Shipping, Supply Chain, Transport and Logistics" implemented in the Action "Reinforcement of the Research and Innovation Infrastructure", funded by the Operational Programme "Competitiveness, Entrepreneurship and Innovation" (NSRF 2014–2020) and co-financed by Greece and the European Regional Development Fund.

References

[1] Sartzetaki M. Value based management analysis framework towards transport enterprises resilience. International Journal of Economics, Business and Management Research. 2019;**3**(6):82-96

[2] Fernández-Muñiz B, Montes-Peón JM, Vázquez-Ordás CJ. Occupational risk management under the OHSAS 18001 standard: Analysis of perceptions and attitudes of certified firms. Journal of Cleaner Production. 2012;**24**:36-47

[3] Hoyle D. ISO 9000 Quality Systems Handbook. 4th ed. Oxford: Butterworth-Heinemann; 2001

[4] Dimitriou D. Corporate planning and management challenges towards business development of European airports. International Journal of Economics, Business and Management Research. 2017;**1**(04):137-148. ISSN: 2456-7760

[5] Dimitriou D. Economic assessment methodology to support decisions for transport infrastructure development. International Journal of Social, Behavioral, Educational, Economic, Business and Industrial Engineering. 2017;**11**(6):1607-1611

[6] Dimitriou D, Sartzetaki M, Kalenteridou I. Dual-level evaluation framework for airport user's satisfaction. International Journal of Operations Research and Information Systems (IJORIS), IGI. 2021;**12**(1):1-14. DOI: 10.4018/IJORIS.2021010102

[7] International Standardization Organization (ISO). ISO 8402 Standard: Quality Management and Quality Assurance—Vocabulary. Geneva: 1994

[8] International Standardization Organization (ISO). ISO 9000 Standard: Quality Management. Geneva: 2000

[9] International Standardization Organization (ISO). ISO 9001: 2015 Standard: Quality Management Systems—Requirements. Geneva: 2015

[10] Kania A, Spilka M. Analysis of integrated management system of the quality, environment and occupational safety. Journal of Achievements in Materials and Manufacturing Engineering. 2016;**78**(2):78-84

[11] International Finance Corporation. Environmental, Health, and Safety (EHS) Guidelines, General EHS Guidelines: Occupational Health and Safety. 2007

[12] Kafel P. The place of occupational health and safety management system in the integrated management system. International Journal for Quality Research. 2016;**10**(2):311-324

[13] Kleinová R, Szaryszová P. The new health and safety standard ISO 45001: 2016 and its planned changes. International Journal of Interdisciplinarity in Theory and Practice, ITPB-NR.: 3. 2014;**2014**:43-47

[14] Lo CKY, Pagellb M, Fana D, Wiengartenc F, Yeungda ACL. OHSAS 18001 certification and operating performance: The role of complexity and coupling. Journal of Operations Management. 2014;**32**(2014):268-280

[15] OHSAS Project Group. Occupational health and Safety Management Systems—Requirements. 2007. ICS 03.100.01; 13.100

[16] OHSAS Project Group. Occupational Health and Safety Management Systems—Guidelines for the Implementation of OHSAS 18001:2007. 2008. ICS 03.100.01: 13.100

[17] Kauppila O, Härkönen J, Väyrynen S. Integrated HSEQ

management systems: Developments and trends. International Journal for Quality Research. 2015;**9**(2):231-242

[18] Majerník M, Lenka Š, Artur K. Quality management in the integrated system as a tool for business excellence and sustainability. International Journal of Interdisciplinarity in Theory and Practice, ITPB-NR.: 3. 2014, 2014;**1**: 10-15. ISSN 2344-2409

[19] Muzaimi H, Chew BC, Hamid SR. Integrated management system: The integration of ISO 9001, ISO 14001, OHSAS 18001 and ISO 31000. In: Engineering International Conference (EIC), AIP Conference Proceedings. 2016. pp. 3-14

[20] Dimitriou D. Evaluation of corporate social responsibility performance in air transport enterprise. Journal of Public Administration and Governance. 2020;**10**(2):262-278. DOI: 10.5296/jpag.v10i2.16645

[21] Dimitriou D., Sartzetaki M. Assessment framework to develop and manage regional intermodal transport networks. Research in Transportation Business & Management. 2020;**35**. p. 100455. DOI: 10.1016/j.rtbm.2020. 100455

Chapter 3

Deep Learning Network for Classifying Target of Same Shape using RCS Time Series

Abstract

The main intension of this work is to find the warhead and decoy classification and identification. Classification of radar target is one of the utmost imperatives and hardest practical problems in finding out the missile. Detection of target in the pool of decoys and debris is one of the major radas technologies widely used in practice. In this study we mainly focus on the radar target recognition in different shapes like cone, cylinder and sphere based on radar cross section (RCS). RCS is a critical element of the radar signature that is used in this work to identify the target. The concept is to focus on new technique of ML for analyzing the input data and to attain a better accuracy. Machine learning has had a significant impact on the entire industry as a result of its high computational competency for target prediction with precise data analysis. We investigated various machine learning classifiers methods to categorize available radar target data. This chapter summarizes conventional and deep learning technique used for classification of radar target.

Keywords: Convolution neural organization (CNN), Recurrent Neural Network (RNN), Support Vector Machine (SVM), High Resolution Range (HRR), Radar Cross Section (RCS), Target classification

1. Introduction

Many countries have spent significant resources to countermeasure research and development in order to condense the efficacy of defense mechanism of Ballistic Missile systems. Using decoys in large number, or fake targets, to ambiguous defense systems is one of the most prevalent tactics. Various decoy tactics, such as replica decoys, signature diversity decoys, and anti-simulation decoys, are currently accessible. Because the weight of payload determines missile's warhead size and range, lightweight decoys are a very interesting choice in contrast to exo-atmospheric defenses. As a result, missiles can carry lightweight decoys in larger number without compromising the maximum range of the payload [1]. In exo-atmospheric in which mid-course phase of a BM flight occurs is the longest part of the journey. Since warhead and decoys travel on comparable trajectories due to same physics a large number of decoys are deployed in midcourse phase [2]. Missiles can release accompanying debris and hardware, such as missile launch boosters, which can cause further radar interference. Since anti-ballistic missile systems are equipped with few numbers of interceptors, In the absence of accurate target identification, it is challenging for anti ballistic missile system to avoid the warhead from reaching its intended target The classification challenge of targets, which involves recognizing the warhead among a larger number of decoys and debris, is critical. So, the need of the hour is to have the desired classification algorithm with high efficiency, low computational complexity and swift decision times for defense radar station. Furthermore, once the target has been classified and located, the seeker on the interceptor must regulate the target location on the vehicle on re-entry for successful lethal supervision and control during the rendezvous [3]. It is crucial to highlight that decoy can have a substantial impact on the efficiency of a defense system in two ways. If a decoy is mistakenly identified as a warhead, the defense may run out of interceptor ammunition too rapidly (false alert).On the other hand, misclassification (seepage) of a weapon may result in its destruction.

Because of the developed target credentialing system based on the distinct micro-motions produced by Ballistic targets, the capacity to discriminate between warheads and decoys has attracted a lot of attention in the literature. Organize their planned ballistic trajectories while demonstrating precession and parapet motion caused by the Earth's gravitational pull [3–5]. On the other hand, due to lack of spinning engine and also due to gravity decoys flip when launched by missiles [6, 7]. In order to obtain the target's micromotion, the radar signals are analyzed using Doppler and range analysis. The phenomena were first described in the Doppler domain by V. Chen in [8], and it is now known as the micro-Doppler effect. Neural network algorithms are extensively used for classification, Deep learning (DL) is a subset of a larger family of data representation-based machine learning algorithms. An observation (such as an image) can be represented in a variety of ways, such as a vector of intensity values per pixel, or more abstractly as a set of edges, specified shape regions, and so on. In [3] Convolution Neural Network (CNN) for classifying aircraft target using LeNet was presented and compared with SVM. The author [6] describes the classification of target using recurrent neural network (RNN) [9–11].

1.1 Ballistic missiles

Missile are the main threats that defense systems have been developed to fight. Initially Ballistic missiles are propelled by rockets, but eventually track the path of targets. They are categorized based on the missile range. To increase the range of a missile, rockets are piled over each other in a staging conformation.

The ballistic missiles categorized in to four categories based on the range it travels it covers:

1. Ballistic missile covering a range less than 1000 kilometers are known as Short range Ballistic missile;

2. Missiles covering a range between 1,000–3,000 kilometers are called as Medium Range Ballistic missile;

3. Ballistic missiles covering a range of 3,000–5,500 kilometers are refereed as Intermediate-range Ballistic missile;and

4. Advanced Ballistic missile covering a range over 5,500 kilometers are called Intercontinental ballistic missiles (ICBMs)

1.2 Ballistic missile launch occurs in three flight stages

Boost phase:

During boost phase missile will be launched and this phase last till the rocket shuts its engine. When rocket shuts its engine, missile is pushed away from Earth. This phase will last anywhere from three to five minutes. The missile moves slowly in general, but an advanced ICBM can achieve speeds of over 6.6 kilometers per sec. Generally this phase takes place in the air (endo-atmospheric).

Midcourse phase:

Upon successful completion of Boost phase missile enters the midcourse phase where in which the missile is over a Ballistic trajectory in the direction of its target. This phase is the longest among the three stages lasting up to 20 min for ICBM. Midcourse phase is divided into two subphases one is the rising phase where missile is moving towards its apogee, in later stage missile is moving towards the earth. During this stage, the missile's warhead(s) and any decoys disengage from the conveyance platform, or "bus." This phase takes place in exo-atmospheric. For the warhead, a reentry vehicle has been requested (RV).

Phase of completion:

The terminal phase begins when the missile's warhead reenters the Earth's atmosphere and lasts until impact or detonation. For a tactical warhead traveling at speeds of more than 0.88 kilometers per sec, this phase takes less than a minute [12].

2. Radar cross section

During the midcourse threat missiles releases its warhead and decoys together, however ground based radar begins tracking the threat in cloud of decoys. Based on the information from radar in the form of RCS returns. Ground based radar classifying using one of the several methods to classify the warhead in the pool of decoys. After classification Ground based radar launches one or more interceptor. The intercept holds kill vehicle. Kill vehicle determines which object is the warhead based on the shape of warhead, it then steers itself into the path of warhead and destroy it with the force of impact. In this section of the chapter, we define Radar Cross section of the target with different shapes. Considering Monostatic pulsed Radar. The RCS of a target is the area that the radar signal intercept.

Mathematically, it is written as:

$$\sigma = \lim_{R\to\infty} 4\pi \frac{|E_s|^2}{|E_i|^2} R^2 \tag{1}$$

Where:

R = Distance traveled by the radar signal to target

E_s = Electric field strength scattered at target.

E_i = Incident electric field strength at target.

2.1 RCS of cylinder and cone

The aspect angle, wavelength of operation and polarization are few parameters determines RCS of a target. When the dimension of the target exceeds the wavelength, the RCS of a conducting plate is approximated by σ.

The product is given by:

$$\sigma = G_e.Ap = \frac{4\pi Ap}{\lambda^2}.\text{Ap} = \frac{4\pi A^2}{\lambda^2} \tag{2}$$

The approximate formula for the RCS of simple cylinder and cone is given by:
Cone RCS:

$$\sigma = \frac{\lambda^2}{16\pi} tan^4\theta; \tag{3}$$

where θ_{cone} half angle.
Cylinder RCS:

$$\sigma = \frac{2\pi a L^2}{\lambda} \text{ where a : Radius; L : Length} \tag{4}$$

3. Classical techniques for radar target identification

The boost, midcourse, and reentry phases of a ballistic missile's flight can be split into three categories. The midcourse begins once the boosters have been turned off. The warhead detaches from the rocket and decoys are released. Because the midcourse may account for 80–90% of the total flight time [1, 13], identifying and intercepting the warhead is a critical phase for the BMD system. However, identifying warheads from decoys is challenging due to their nearly identical macro-motions [2]. To maintain attitude control, the warhead spins in mid-flight. The warhead's micro-motion becomes spinning and processing at a miniscule nutation angle as a result of the inevitable tumbling. After initial tumbling, Wang [3] revealed that an axisymmetric decoy's micromotion spins and processes, similar to a warhead, but with a higher nutation angle. The most difficult difficulty in this study is distinguishing between a warhead and a decoy of identical shape in mid-flight, with the sole difference being micro-motion.

In radar target recognition, there are a plethora of ways (RATR). This section of the chapter discusses different methods.

The trajectory of the intercontinental ballistic missile's midcourse is essentially dual-body motion.

The fundamental equation for dual-body motion is:

$$r^n + \frac{\mu}{|r|^3} r = 0 \tag{5}$$

Where geocentric distance vector represented as r^n with order two, the earth's gravitational constant denoted as μ.

3.1 Micromotion feature

Various types of targets have dissimilar friction features during trajectory operation. In the fretting characteristics of warheads, angular velocity is taken into account, as is swing in the fretting characteristics of heavy baits, and random frequency roll in the fretting features of light baits, boosters and also fragment groups. The warhead rotates in a vector direction while spinning around its own symmetry axis. Precession is the name given to this period of rotation. The angle of precession is the angle formed by the axis of symmetry and the vector's direction (**Figure 1**).

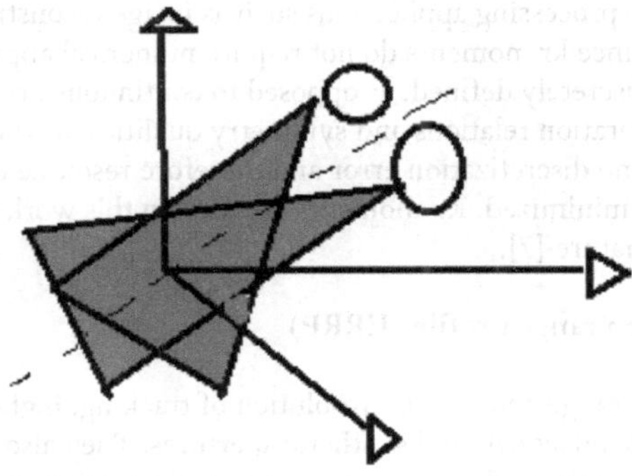

Figure 1.
Warhead precession model.

The orbit causes the bait to swing in a vertical plane, and the difference of the swing angle is $\theta = \theta(t) = \theta_s \sin \omega_s t$ Where θ_s is is the swing amplitude the and ω_s swing angle frequency.

The target acquisition with dynamic RCS sequence is influenced by attitude angle. Altitude is the angle between line of sight of the radar and target axis. Using the sequence of attitude angles, the target static RCS library, target dynamic RCS sequence can be obtained [14].

3.2 Trajectory information

The author of this paper described a technique for quickly identifying a warhead during boost phase by combining kinematic information obtained from the target's trajectory through an enhanced Kalman filter by means of a constant jerk model. During the boost phase, the main factors influence on the missile are engine thrust along with gravity, and air resistance, with engine thrust being the most potent. After separation, the warhead and the wreckage of the uncontrolled components have a significant difference. Although the warhead speeds, the wreckage does not. Because the missile is flying at a low angle of attack, the thrust acceleration is nearly parallel to the ground during the boost phase. As a result, during the boost phase the warhead acceleration on velocity is rather substantial. Once the wreckage has been separated, gravity and air resistance are the main forces act on it. However, as the rubble falls, it can be enjoyable after a while. As a result, the target's upward velocity component and the projection of acceleration on velocity are chosen as the recognition method's two properties. To obtain more precise target motion data, an extended Kalman filter with constant jerk model is utilized, which improves recognition performance by lowering the impact of radar measurement noise [6, 15].

3.3 Radar cross-section (RCS) time series, micro-Doppler information

Because warheads and ambiguous objects exhibit a variety of micro-motions throughout their ballistic trajectory, the micro-Doppler effect analysis, which was presented and has been extensively studied in recent years was utilized to generate reliable information for target detection. While precession and nutation define warhead flight, the intriguing objects just wobble due to the lack of a phase motor control. When analyzing the gathered radar data, these various micro-motions result in diverse micro-Doppler fingerprints. A unique feature extraction strategy based on Krawtchouk (Kr) moments is proposed in this research for ballistic target categorization. Because of their unique properties, Kr-moments are commonly employed in image processing applications such as image reconstruction, shape and face recognition. Since kr moments do not require numerical approximation because they are discretely defined, as opposed to continuous orthogonal moments. Because of the reiteration relations and symmetry qualities of Krawtchouk moments, there is no discretization error and therefore resource essential to store the polynomials is minimized. Kr-moments are used in this work for analyzing micro-doppler signature [7].

3.4 High-resolution range profile (HRRP)

To improve the range and angular resolution of tracking, high-resolution radars (HRRs) use broadband signals and synthetic apertures. They also provide, two or more -dimensional high-resolution scans carrying information about the intended characteristic of the target, which can be used to exactly classify and identify the targets. Range-Doppler imaging, phase-derived ranging, and micro-motion characteristics are all obtained using advanced signal processing methods in HRRs. However, issues such as reduced SNR and tracking precision of multi-scatter point targets limit the benefits and applications of HRRs. The author explains the novel HRR technologies and addresses the difficulties and keys related to detection, tracking, imaging in this study. Lastly, it examines the most recent developments and representative findings from HRR-based research [8]. The target signature's inverse Radon transform is characterized by a high-resolution range profile frame collected inside a full period of the target's key rotation, is computed in this study to provide a new approach for the categorization of ballistic targets. The precession of warheads and the tumbling of decoys are also considered. The classifier's final feature vector is determined by the pseudo-Zernike moments of the subsequent transformation. The extracted features ensure resilience contrary to the target's size and velocity of rotation, as well as the target's beginning motion phase [5, 16, 17].

3.5 Images from synthetic aperture radar (SAR)

For synthetic aperture radar (SAR) target detection, a multi-criteria sparse depiction-based classification (SRC) is devised. To generate the coefficient vector throughout the global dictionary sparse representation is applied. As a result, categorization is based on three alternative choice criteria: minimum global and local reconstruction reconstruction errors, and maximum coefficient energy. Each of the three rules approaches the coefficient vector in a unique way, allowing them to complement one another. After performing a linear combination on the three outcomes using an adaptive weighting approach, a final judgment is made [18–21].

4. Depp learning technique for radar target identification

Decoys, debris, and trash are frequently convoy near the real warhead during the midcourse of a ballistic missile to boost the missile's penetrating capacity. This interferes with the identification of the real warhead via radar. Since absence of atmospheric drag, the fake targets approach the warhead at a high rate, producing a target assembly. Their macro motions remain same, but their micro motions differ, resulting in RCS time sequence differences. This is the foundation to distinguish between real and false targets.

Deep neural networks (DNNs) have recently been a prevalent study topic in classification. DNNs can learn high-level depictions from large datasets, proceeding with the state of the art in a range of challenging problems and fields. In image classification, language understanding, speech recognition, and a number of other domains. This will enable DNNs to be used successfully in a wider range of fields. Deep recurrent neural networks, deep feed-forward neural networks, and convolutional neural networks are some of the several types of DNNs.

4.1 Recurrent neural network

The capacity of RNNs to function with conceptual classifications is well-known. The RNN can recall previous time step outputs and use them to make judgments for the current step. The RNNs' chain structure suggests that they can be used intuitively with sequences. The current time-step input in an RNN is made up of new data and the total network's output from the previous time-step. As demonstrated in **Figure 2**, any gradient-based optimization strategy used to train an RNN may encounter the vanishing gradient issue at some time [9]. Furthermore, if data from multiple time steps or more is required before making a decision by the current time step, it may be unable to provide a precise prediction. 'Long ShortTerm Memory' (LSTM) is a technique that helps to solve this issue [10, 11]. The vanishing gradient problem is addressed in the LSTM by incorporating three gated units: a forget, input and output, and a forget gate respectively [9–11, 22, 23].

Conventional RNN is shown in **Figure 2**, the RNN is defined as

$$h_k = \varphi_h\left(w^{hi} i_k + w^{hh} h_{k-1}\right) \tag{6}$$

$$o_k = \varphi_o\left(w^{oh} h_k\right) \tag{7}$$

4.2 Convolution neural network

Like a standard multilayer neural network, a Convolutional Neural Network (CNN) is made up of multiple convolutional layers followed by multiple fully linked layers. The CNN architecture is intended to take use of the 2D structure of a picture. To provide translation invariant features, resident connections and weights are used, followed by some sort of pooling. With the lesser parameters than fully linked networks with the similar number of hidden units makes CNNs easier to train. A m X m X r picture is used as the input to a convolutional layer, where m is the image's height and breadth and number of channels is denoted by r. The k filters of size o X o X q constitute the convolutional layer, where 'o' is less than the image's dimension and q may be similar as or less than the number of channels r, and even may vary for each kernel. Filters size creates connected structures are then

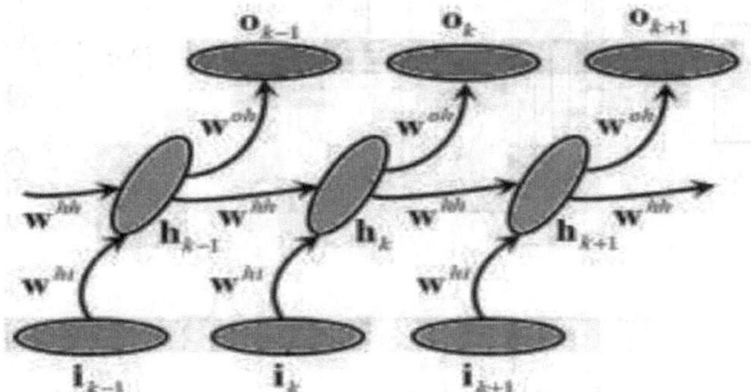

Figure 2.
Recurrent neural network consists of input, hidden and output layer.

convolved with the picture to create k feature maps of size m-o + 1. Each map is then subsampled using mean or maximum pooling over p X p connecting regions, with p ranging from 2 for small images to 5 for bigger images.

Before or after the subsampling layer, each feature map is given additive bias and sigmoidal nonlinearity. **Figure 3** shows a typical convolutional neural network architecture, which includes two convolutional layers, two maximum pooling layers, and one fully connected layer.

CNN structure with one dimensionality was designed for warhead and decoy classification based on RCS time series based on ten missile paths are simulated, each with the same shape warhead and decoy but varied micro-motion [24]. RCSnet, a 1D convolutional neural network structure that employs the radar cross-section (RCS) time series to identify warhead and decoy targets of the same form in mid-flight, was presented. On a simulation dataset, it was compared to 5 typical classification methods that utilized 26 selected features [19, 25].

The SCF signature pattern classification approach uses a noise-resilient and unique 2-D signature pattern formed by the spectral correlation function (SCF) and a robust deep belief network (DBN) deep learning algorithm. The radar system was set up in a lab setting, information was acquired for three micro UASs, and the data was used to test the signal processing technique [26]. For detection of sea-surface targets, a faster region-based convolutional neural network (Faster R-CNN) was developed. It uses a deep convolutional network to extract visual features and detects them using the "selective search + CNN + SVM" method. R-CNN training takes a long time and takes up a lot of disc space [21, 23, 27].

4.3 Support vector machine

SVM works by determining the best classification hyperplane that meets the classification criteria and optimizes the margin areas on both sides of the hyperplane while preserving classification precision. SVM algorithms include linear branched support vector machines, linear support vector machines, and non-linear support vector machines. If the input space has non-linear separability, an appropriate non-linear mapping is used to move the sample points from the input space to

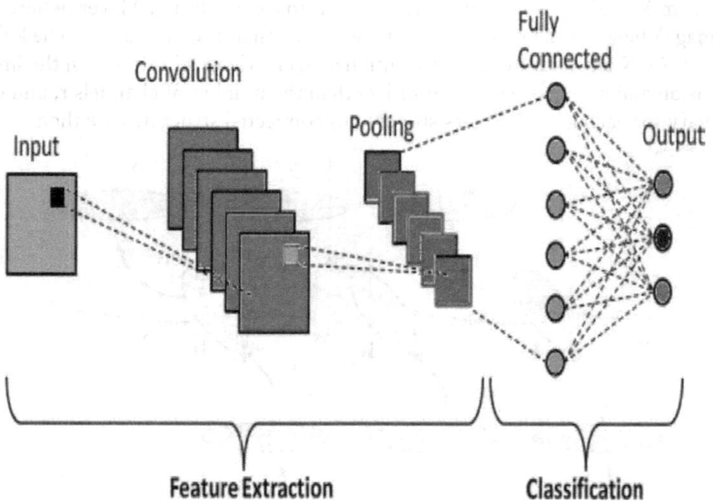

Figure 3.
Architecture of convolutional neural network.

References	Method	Findings
[22]	RNN: Using Physical optics RCS data for all possible aspect angle and elevation are estimated	Open-source tool called POFACETS used for creating RCS database as a function of aspect angles. This technique provides 95% accuracy using the data based created. But not suitable for the noisy condition.
[28]	Target dynamics are modeled, target is treated as appoint object	Sates estimation accuracy is not sensitive to the maneuvers and quantitative analysis is difficult due to the involvement of convex optimization
[24]	MSTAR data set consisting of 10 military target SAR images	Feature extraction by constructing a multistage network to learn SAR images. High computational complexity and delay is processing is observed.
[25]	CNN	Training time using RCSnet is longer than conventional method. Not suitable for real time application.
[29]	SVM	Statistical feature extracted from RCS time series. This method is more sensitive to the number of samples and unstable for larger data set

Table 1.
References with method and findings were summarized.

a high-dimensional feature space, resulting in linear separability in the feature space for the corresponding sample points.

The motion trajectory and micromotion features of seven different types of targets are combined to mimic dynamic RCS sequences of diverse targets. The above data is then used to extract 10 statistical features with separation qualities, such as position feature, distribution feature, and transform domain feature parameters. In a complicated scenario, the SVM method is used to classify and detect multitargets (**Table 1**) [29].

5. Summary

The main aim of this work is to find the warhead and decoy classification and identification. Classification of radar target is one of the utmost imperative and hardest practical problems in finding out the missile. Detection of target in the pool of decoys and debris is one of the major radar technology widely used in practice. In this study we mainly focus on the radar target recognition in different shapes like cone, cylinder and sphere based on radar cross section (RCS). RCS is a critical element of the radar signature that is used in this work to identify the target. The concept is to focus on new technique of ML for analyzing the input data and to attain a better accuracy. Machine learning has had a significant impact on the entire industry as a result of its high computational competency for target prediction with precise data analysis. Among the Various ML techniques, convolutional neural networks perform better than support vector machine.

Conflict of interest

The authors declare no conflict of interest.

References

[1] Fetter, S., Sessler, A. M., Cornwall, J. M., Dietz, B., Frankel, S., Garwin, R. L., ... & Wright, D. C. (2000). Countermeasures: a technical evaluation of the operational effectiveness of the planned US national missile defense system.

[2] Gao, H., Xie, L., Wen, S., & Kuang, Y. (2010). Micro-Doppler signature extraction from ballistic target with micro-motions. IEEE Transactions on Aerospace and Electronic Systems, 46 (4), 1969-1982.

[3] Lei, P., & Liu, Y. X. (2012, October). Feature extraction and target recognition of missile targets based on micro-motion. In 2012 IEEE 11th International Conference on Signal Processing (Vol. 3, pp. 1914-1919). IEEE.

[4] Persico, A. R., Ilioudis, C. V., Clemente, C., Soraghan, J. J. "Novel classification algorithm for ballistic target based on HRRP frame", 'Institute of Electrical and Electronics Engineers (IEEE)', 2019

[5] Teng Long, Zhennan Liang, Quanhua Liu. "Advanced technology of high-resolution radar: target detection, tracking, imaging, and recognition", Science China Information Sciences, 2019

[6] Chen, J., Xu, S., Tian, B., Wu, J., & Chen, Z. (2015). A fast recognition method of warhead target in boost phase using kinematic features. MIPPR 2015: Automatic Target Recognition and Navigation. doi:10.1117/12.2207401.

[7] Persico, A. R., Clemente, C., Pallotta, L., De Maio, A., & Soraghan, J. (2016). Micro-Doppler classification of ballistic threats using Krawtchouk moments. 2016 IEEE Radar Conference (RadarConf). doi:10.1109/radar.2016.7485086

[8] Long, T., Liang, Z. & Liu, Q. Advanced technology of high-resolution radar: target detection, tracking, imaging, and recognition. Sci. China Inf. Sci. 62, 40301 (2019).

[9] Gao, C., Liu, H., Zhou, S., Su, H., Chen, B., Yan, J., & Yin, K. (2018, August). Maneuvering target tracking with recurrent neural networks for radar application. In 2018 International Conference on Radar (RADAR) (pp. 1-5). IEEE.

[10] Bhattacharyya, Kaustubh & Sarma, Kandarpa. (2012). Automatic Target Recognition (ATR) System using Recurrent Neural Network (RNN) for Pulse Radar. International Journal of Computer Applications. 50. 10.5120/7960-1154.

[11] Wang, L., Tang, J., & Liao, Q. (2019). A Study on Radar Target Detection Based on Deep Neural Networks. IEEE Sensors Letters, 1–1. doi:10.1109/lsens.2019.2896072

[12] www.armscontrol.org

[13] Persico, A. R., Clemente, C., Gaglione, D., Ilioudis, C. V., Cao, J., Pallotta, L., ... & Soraghan, J. J. (2017). On model, algorithms, and experiment for micro-Doppler-based recognition of ballistic targets. IEEE Transactions on Aerospace and Electronic Systems, 53 (3), 1088-1108.

[14] Wenbo Tang, Lei Yu, Yinsheng Wei, Peng Tong. "Radar Target Recognition of Ballistic Missile in Complex Scene", 2019 IEEE International Conference on Signal, Information and Data Processing (ICSIDP), 2019.

[15] Chen, Jian, Shiyou Xu, Biao Tian, Jianhua Wu, and Zengping Chen. "A fast recognition method of warhead target in boost phase using kinematic features",

MIPPR 2015 Automatic Target Recognition and Navigation, 2015

[16] A. R. Persico, C. V. Ilioudis, C. Clemente and J. J. Soraghan, "Novel Classification Algorithm for Ballistic Target Based on HRRP Frame," in IEEE Transactions on Aerospace and Electronic Systems, vol. 55, no. 6, pp. 3168-3189, Dec. 2019, doi: 10.1109/TAES.2019.2905281.

[17] Bharat Sehgal, Hanumant Singh Shekhawat, Sumit Kumar Jana. "Automatic Target Recognition Using Recurrent Neural Networks", 2019 International Conference on Range Technology (ICORT), 2019

[18] Junhua Wang & Yongping Zhai (2021) Target recognition of synthetic aperture radar images using multi-criteria SRC, Remote Sensing Letters, 12: 8, 739-749, DOI: 10.1080/2150704X.2021.1934594

[19] Ali El Housseini, Abdelmalek Toumi, Ali Khenchaf. "Deep Learning for target recognition from SAR images", 2017 Seminar on Detection Systems Architectures and Technologies (DAT), 2017

[20] Junhua Wang, Yongping Zhai. "Target recognition of synthetic aperture radar images using multi-criteria SRC", Remote Sensing Letters, 2021

[21] weaponsandwarfare.com

[22] Sehgal, B., Shekhawat, H. S., & Jana, S. K. (2019). Automatic Target Recognition Using Recurrent Neural Networks. 2019 International Conference on Range Technology (ICORT). doi:10.1109/icort46471.2019.9069656

[23] Li Wang, Jun Tang, Qingmin Liao. "A Study on Radar Target Detection Based on Deep Neural Networks", IEEE Sensors Letters, 2019.

[24] Jiang, W., Ren, Y., Liu, Y. et al. A method of radar target detection based on convolutional neural network. Neural Comput & Applic 33, 9835–9847 (2021). https://doi.org/10.1007/s00521-021-05753-w

[25] Carrera, E. V., Lara, F., Ortiz, M., Tinoco, A., & Leon, R. (2020). Target Detection using Radar Processors based on Machine Learning. 2020 IEEE ANDESCON. doi:10.1109/andescon50619.2020.9272173

[26] Chen, Jian & Shiyou, Xu & Chen, Zengping. (2018). Convolutional neural network for classifying space target of the same shape by using RCS time series. IET Radar, Sonar & Navigation. 12. 10.1049/iet-rsn.2018.5237.

[27] Yan, H., Chen, C., Jin, G., Zhang, J., Wang, X., & Zhu, D. (2021). Implementation of a Modified Faster R-CNN for Target Detection Technology of Coastal Defense Radar. Remote Sensing, 13(9), 1703.

[28] T. Tang, C. Wang and M. Gao, "Radar Target Recognition Based on Micro-Doppler Signatures Using Recurrent Neural Network," 2021 IEEE 4th International Conference on Electronics Technology (ICET), 2021, pp. 189-194, doi: 10.1109/ICET51757.2021.9450934.

[29] W. Tang, L. Yu, Y. Wei and P. Tong, "Radar Target Recognition of Ballistic Missile in Complex Scene," 2019 IEEE International Conference on Signal, Information and Data Processing (ICSIDP), 2019, pp. 1-6, doi: 10.1109/ICSIDP47821.2019.9172943.

Chapter 4

Behavioral Modeling Paradigm for More Electric Aircraft Power Electronic Converters

Abstract

To control the power flow among various energy sources and loads of a power system of modern more electric aircrafts, power electronics converters are employed. The integration of multiple sources into distribution system and their interconnection with variety of loads through power electronic converters results in a complex dynamic system. Modeling of these systems prior to implementation becomes necessary to analyze and predict system's behavior. The classical modeling approaches require detail knowledge about the topology and parameters of the active and passive components of the power electronics converters. While in modern system, most of the power electronics converters are ready to use power electronics modules. These modules come from different manufacturers, lacking the necessary information to build the conventional switch or average models. The chapter would cover dynamic behavioral modeling technique for power electronics systems to be employed in more electric aircrafts, which do not require any prior information about the internal details of the system.

Keywords: behavioral modeling, two port network, power electronic converters, system identification, more electric aircraft

1. Introduction

The ever increasing consumption and growing demand for reliable supply of electrical energy has led the electrical engineers to do more research in the field of distributed energy systems (DES). A distributed energy system delivers power to different electrical and electronic loads, by conventional as well as number of renewable energy sources, e.g. solar energy, wind energy, bio mass, fuel cells etc. With the availability of these resources comes the issue of their integration into existing power distribution system. Thanks to the advancement in power electronics technology, which has enabled the power distribution systems to supply various loads not only from the traditional utility grid but also from modern alternative energy sources. The recent trend of shift in power distribution systems from centralized architecture to distributed architecture has led to a significant increase in the number of power electronics converters being employed in these power distribution systems. The conventional power systems based upon a centralized architecture have only a single source delivering power to various loads [1–3].

The conventional power systems are being replaced with more advanced distributed energy systems for various applications, in which loads are supplied by multiple energy sources through a number of power electronics converters, distributed throughout the system [4–10]. These hybrid energy systems include more than one source of energy, energy storage elements and active and passive loads, either dc, ac or both. This implies the use of power electronics converters, to control the power flow over the entire system, hence also called electronic power distribution system (EPDS). It illustrates that in future EPDS the dynamics of electrical energy generation, distribution and consumption will be dynamically decoupled through the use of power electronics converters. In the literature, the distributed energy systems have been discussed for most of the modern state of the art applications, i.e. more electric aircrafts (MEA) [11], more electric vehicles (MEV)/hybrid more electric vehicles (HMEV) [12], all electric ships (AES) [13], telecommunication systems and data communication systems [3, 14], and for commercial and residential systems [15, 16].

The integration of multiple sources into distributed energy system and their interconnection with variety of loads through power electronics converters in more electric aircrafts results in a complex dynamic system [17]. Therefore, it becomes necessary to model these systems prior to implementation for analysis and prediction of system's behavior [4, 13, 18–21]. The requirement to model power converters for system level analysis was first discussed in [18], and subsequent work has been done in this direction in [4, 13, 19]. However, the pre-requisite for all of the classical modeling approaches regarding the analysis of the overall system is to have complete knowledge about the topology and parameters of the power electronics converters and other subsystems employed [20–23]. In more electric aircrafts, most of the power electronics converters used are ready to use power electronics modules. The issue commonly faced is that, different modules such as converters, filters and loads are designed by different vendors and lack the necessary information required to build the conventional switch or average models. **Figure 1** shows a commercial dc-dc converter [24] which serves as a ready to be employed power electronics module.

This leads us to the behavioral or black-box modeling approach, which does not require any prior information about the topology and parameters of the system and hence is very effective for modeling different power electronics converters based systems. The behavioral modeling concept is based upon the measurement of a set of *g*-parameters, which are obtained via performing certain measurements at only the input–output terminals of the converter. The dynamic behavioral models developed using this approach are able to predict the transient as well as steady state behavior of the system.

Figure 1.
Commercial dc-dc power electronics converter module.

2. Overview of power distribution systems

In the literature, two most popular power distribution approaches have been centralized approach and distributed approach. A brief overview is given here.

2.1 Centralized power architecture

The conventional power systems are mostly based upon a centralized architecture. The centralized power systems have only a single power electronics converter delivering power to various loads. **Figure 2** shows the conventional centralized power distribution architecture for a typical telecommunication system. The -48 V bus is supplied by the ac-dc converter and battery storage is used as back up. In this case a single dc-dc converter delivers power to several loads through various output busses.

The biggest drawback of such centralized power systems is that they lack reliability, i.e. in case the single intermediate converter fails, the whole system will shut down.

2.2 Distributed power architecture

In distributed energy systems, loads are supplied by a number of different power converters which are distributed throughout the system. In contrast to centralized power architecture the distributed power architecture offers several advantages. The distributed power system (DPS) offers improved reliability in terms that if one of the converter fails, the whole system will not shut down. The parallel connected converters on the load side provide the option of immediate replacement of any damaged module, while keeping the rest of the system operational.

The aircraft power systems are also undergoing a great change by moving towards more electric aircraft, adopting distributed architecture. The conventional power sources such as pneumatic, hydraulic and mechanical are being replaced with electrical power. The MEA concept promises to improve the reliability and efficiency of the overall system and at the same time reducing the weight and size of the equipment [11, 12, 25].

The researchers have come up with various proposals for MEA technology implementation. One of the proposal is based upon variable frequency 230 V_{AC} bus as shown in **Figure 3** [26]. The traditional constant frequency generator is being replaced with variable frequency generator. The auto transformer rectifier unit (ATRU) and pulse width modulation (PWM) rectifier are in cascade with inverters to feed the motors. Singe phase ac loads are connected to the bus through power factor correction (PFC) circuits. The 28 V_{DC} bus is connected to the variable frequency ac bus through transformer rectifier unit (TRU) and dc-dc converter, which are then connected to a backup dc voltage source and various dc loads.

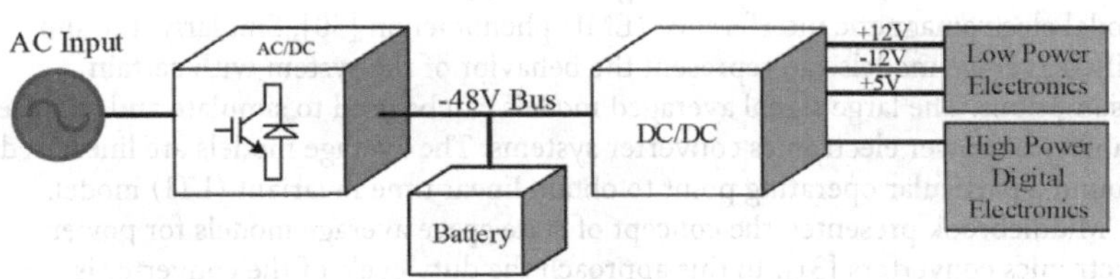

Figure 2.
Conventional centralized power architecture for telecommunication system [3].

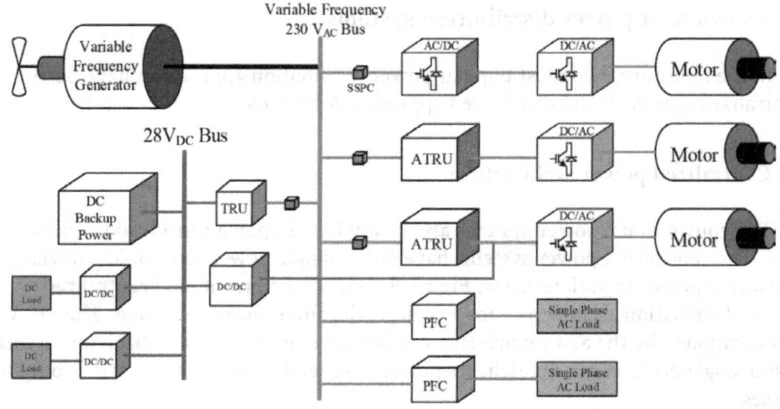

Figure 3.
Distributed power system for MEA using variable frequency ac bus.

As can be seen from above example, there is a shift in power distribution system architecture for more electric aircrafts. In an overall complex network the traditional utility network along with renewable energy sources and storage elements is connected to multiple loads through power electronics converters. The power electronics converters involved are ac-dc, ac-ac, dc-ac and dc-dc. Also these converters can be either unidirectional or bidirectional and have connection configuration of series or parallel, mainly depending upon the application. Therefore, it is required to build models for these power electronics converters which have become a key part of the modern DES for more electric aircrafts.

3. Modeling hierarchy review

As per the above discussion, to simulate and analyze the behavior of a complete system, it is required to develop models for different subsystems. In the literature, modeling of power electronics converters from detailed switching models to very abstract behavioral models has been discussed. A brief review is given here.

3.1 White box models

When all the necessary data to model the system's behavior is available, then in such cases a white-box modeling approach is useful. The switch and average models are types of white-box modeling approach [27, 28]. At converter level, the switch models are the most detailed ones which give the designer an idea about workflow of the circuit during various switching states [29]. These are also used to study and model electromagnetic interference (EMI) phenomenon [30]. Similarly, the simplified average models can represent the behavior of the system with certain assumptions. The large signal averaged models can be used to simulate and analyze stability of power electronics converter systems. The average models are linearized around a particular operating point to obtain linear time invariant (LTI) model.

Middlebrook presented the concept of state space average models for power electronics converters [31]. In this approach the duty cycle of the converter is averaged over one complete period. The average modeling results in a continuous model that ignores the switching action but includes the nonlinear behavior of the converter. In order to apply linear system theory techniques, the average model is linearized around an operating point. The operating point is then used to design the controller for the system and analyze stability of the system. Often the parasitic elements are neglected to simplify the modeling process. Yet the average models provide a good solution for modeling and analysis of the converter. The general form of state space average model for a pulse width modulation (PWM) converter is as given in Eq. (1)

$$\dot{x} = \sum_{i=1}^{n}(A_i d_i x + B_i d_i u) \\ y = (Cx + Du) \tag{1}$$

where x, u and y represent the state, input and output variables respectively, d_i is the duty cycle, and A, B, C, D are system matrices.

Few other modeling techniques in this category are; generalized state space average models [32], discrete average models [33] and cyclic average models [34]. However, state space averaging is most widely used due to its simplicity and good dynamic estimation for most applications.

The averaging techniques have also been applied to three phase ac systems, i.e. ac-ac, ac-dc and dc-ac PWM converters [35]. The average models for three phase systems are transformed to synchronous *dq* reference frame, in which the system is operated at a certain point for the application of small signal modeling techniques. The average modeling of three phase diode and line commutated rectifiers has also been widely investigated [36, 37].

Both in the case of switch as well as average models, the designer has complete information about the topology and parameters of the converter. But the white-box modeling approach fails in case of power electronics modules where the designers do not have any or complete information to build switch or average models.

3.2 Gray box models

Depending upon the system and the information about it, it is possible to approximately write state space equations with unknown parameters which are to be estimated later, this method is called gray box modeling [38]. It is an intermediate case falling between white-box and black-box modeling, where part of the information is available to the designer from the datasheets about the converter topology and internal circuit parameters. Hence part of the model reflects the design of the system while remaining which is numerically modeled serves as black-box. Some reduced order average models also fall within this category.

3.3 Behavioral or black-box models

Behavioral models are mainly not concerned with the detailed internal structure or parameters of the converters. These models are built without requiring any prior information about the internal parameters of the converter and also called black-box models [39, 40]. The term *behavioral modeling* is normally associated with the modeling of such type of converters. It refers to the modeling technique in which models for power electronics converters and passive modules e.g. electromagnetic induction filters are built without any available information about their internal design and components. The models of power electronics converters with minimum or no detail about the system are used to analyze the input–output behavior of the system.

The behavioral modeling of power electronics converters can be broadly classified into linear and non-linear techniques, depending upon the model structure. These techniques are oriented to either converter or system level design and based upon parametric and nonparametric identification methods. The parametric methods describe the system's behavior using transfer function or state space models. These models are identified using either time or frequency domain data. The non-parametric methods describe the system's behavior using impulse response or frequency response data. Also, a non-parametric model can also be used as input for parametric identification such as, frequency response data can be used to identify a transfer function model.

3.3.1 Linear techniques

The very first linear black-box modeling techniques were used to obtain the model of the plant, i.e. from the duty cycle to output voltage response of the converter. The model was then used to design controller for the system. Middlebrook presented the method to experimentally measure the loop gain frequency response through ac sweep signal, which results in a non-parametric black-box model [41]. Later, further work has been done to determine the control to output response of switching converters using either parametric or non-parametric methods. The parametric method is used in [42] to identify coefficients of a discrete difference equation using a pseudo random binary signal (PRBS) as excitation input signal. A non-parametric method is used to identify the frequency response of a converter using impulse response in [43]. An improved nonparametric cross-correlation method of system identification is proposed in [44]. It aims to improve the accuracy of frequency response identification, especially at high frequencies near the optimum closed loop bandwidth frequency. Fourier analysis is applied to the identified impulse response to obtain the small signal frequency response. Linear black-box models have also been used to synthesize controllers for power converters, for which it is difficult to obtain analytical models, i.e. series resonant converter [45].

The system oriented linear behavioral modeling technique has been employed to model components of power system as an input–output network in [46]. The subsystems are modeled as two port linear network using small signal linear average approach. The *g*-parameters as transfer functions are obtained by averaging state-space equations followed by small signal perturbations. Another method to obtain the *g*-parameters is by input–output frequency response measurements followed by parametric identification algorithm.

3.3.2 Non-linear techniques

Most of the power electronics converters are non-linear systems, so the linear techniques are valid only around a particular operating point. The non-linear modeling techniques have been developed to obtain models which are valid for a wide operating range. In order to model the duty cycle to output voltage response for a dc-dc converter, a non-linear autoregressive moving average with exogenous input (NARMAX) model is employed in [47], which consists of a non-linear discrete differential equation. It requires time domain data to identify the model, which is obtained by perturbing the duty cycle and measuring the output voltage. Neural networks have the ability to model non-linear functions which can be related by input–output data for a non-linear system. A neural network is applied to model the control to output voltage behavior of a converter for control design in [48].

Another technique which can be employed when some limited information is available is called, Wiener and Hammerstein approach [49, 50]. These models are valid when the non-linearities are present in the steady state variables only, in case the dynamic part of the system is also affected by non-linearities then this approach fails. **Figure 4** represents Wiener and Hammerstein modeling approach. In these models, the linear block represents dynamic system as transfer function while the non-linear block represents steady state operating point. In Wiener model the linear block precedes the non-linear block and it is opposite in the case of Hammerstein model. The structure of Wiener and Hammerstein models is limited to single input and single output and it also requires time domain data to build the models.

In this dissertation lookup table and polytopic structure based non-linear behavioral modeling methodology has been described, where lookup table based approach has been used for mild non-linearities, while for severely non-linear dynamic relations more complex polytopic structure based approach has been applied.

3.4 System level Modeling

To design modern distributed energy system, which includes number of power electronics modules connected in various configurations, module based behavioral modeling is required for the analysis of the complete system. Two port network utilizing *g*-parameters based converter level modeling was initially applied in [51]. This method was subsequently used to analyze the interaction among subsystems in a networked system [52]. But in this approach first small signal model of the converter is required which is used to derive the *g*-parameters. The small signal modeling requires knowledge about the topology and parameters of the converter, which as mentioned above is often not available to the designer.

To model the large signal behavior of dc-dc converters based upon system identification, a different approach was proposed in [49]. In contrast to *g*-parameters based modeling, it is a circuit oriented approach which partially relies on the data provided in the datasheet. The model is a hybrid Wiener-Hammerstein structure, where the static non-linear block is identified from the data about efficiency, static regulation and thermal characteristics, while the dynamic linear block is identified from the transient response data. This technique was also used to model a nanogrid, where model for each subsystem is divided into two blocks [53].

Modern distributed energy systems are based upon commercial converters [54–56], with lack of information to build conventional white box models.

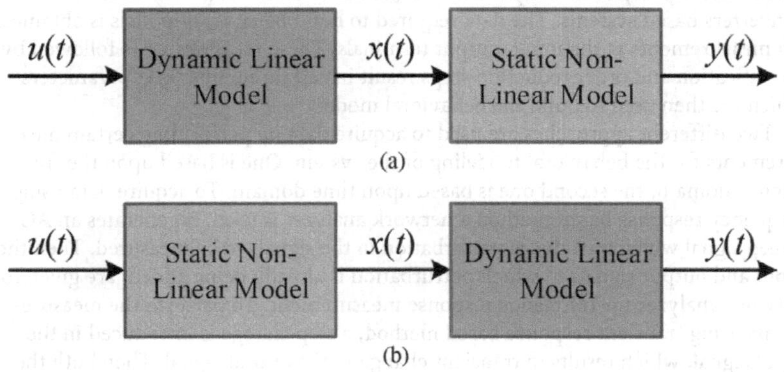

Figure 4.
(a) Wiener and (b) Hammerstein model structures.

Therefore, among various techniques mentioned above g-parameters based behavioral modeling would be most effective [57]. The main advantage of g-parameters based behavioral modeling methodology is that large system can be subdivided into subsystems, then these can be easily combined after modeling resulting in any desired architecture. In order to model each subsystem, the idea is to obtain the parameters that characterize their dynamic behavior of each via accessing only the input–output terminals [58].

4. Current lack in state of the art

To integrate several different power electronics converters as part of electronic power distribution system, it is often required to model in priori and simulate the whole system [4, 13, 18, 20]. It can speed up the design process and reduce the amount of experimental work. Hence, behavioral modeling approach should be adopted to model such converters. There are certain challenges faced during this process which are summarized below:

One problem which arises during behavioral modeling is the high order of the measured g-parameters. The individual models of the converters should be low order and represent only the input–output dynamics, i.e. behavior of the system. So certain technique should be adopted that the behavioral model is not only successfully able to represent the behavior of the system but also is computationally efficient to consume less simulation time.

The behavioral models should cover the entire operating range of the system and predict the dynamic response of the system under small or large signal disturbances either at source or load. But power electronics converters due to their switching action are inherently non-linear systems and behavioral models developed at one operating point are not valid over the wide operating range. Hence non-linear behavioral modeling approach is required to be adopted for such systems, which will enable these models to analyze and predict the response of the system over the entire operating range.

5. Behavioral modeling methodology

This section presents the methodology to build the behavioral models for power electronics converter based systems. In this methodology the dynamic behavioral models are developed to analyze and predict the behavior of power electronics converters based systems. The data required to build behavioral models is obtained via measurements at the input–output terminals. These measurements followed by identification and order reduction steps result in certain number of g-parameters which are then used to build the behavioral model.

Two different approaches are used to acquire data by performing certain measurements for the behavioral modeling of the system. One is based upon the frequency domain, the second one is based upon time domain. To acquire data using frequency response based method a network analyzer is used. It generates an AC sweep signal which introduces perturbation in the signals to be measured. Then the input and output signals to which perturbation is already being added, are given to network analyzer for frequency response measurement. To perform the measurements using transient response based method, a step change is introduced in the input signal, which results in transient change in the output signal. Then both the input and output time domain signals are recorded using an oscilloscope and subsequently used for identification of frequency response.

While the measurements are made, it is ensured that the parameters of the behavioral model completely represent the internal dynamics of the system, excluding any source or load effects. **Figure 5** shows general view of the black-box based two port network representation for the behavioral modeling of a dc-dc converter.

In **Figure 5** the symbols can be generalized as v_j and i_j representing voltage and current, where $j \in (i, o)$, the subscripts i and o represent the input and output terminals respectively.

Once the data is obtained by performing these measurements, then system identification techniques are applied using the simulation package, i.e. MATLAB/SIMULINK [59] to develop the relationship between the specific input and output for which the measurements are recorded. It should be noted that once the data is obtained using either of the two measurement techniques then the processing of data to build models does not require any other information about the converter. The parameters obtained from measurement data acquire all the information required to build behavioral model of the system.

In order to address the issue of high order modeling, Hankel singular values based order reduction technique is employed. In addition a criteria is proposed which determines the number of states required to be retained for the reduced order model. The reduced order model obtained using this approach is not only successfully able to represent the behavior of the system but also is computationally efficient and requires less simulation time.

The verification and validation methodology is used to investigate the behavioral models for power electronics converters based systems. For each case under study, the methodology is first verified via simulation. During this step a simulation model of the system is setup in certain simulation packages, i.e. MATLAB/SIMULINK or SABER [60]. In the next step validation of the system is performed for experimental setup. The experimental setup is based upon certain laboratory made prototypes or

Figure 5.
Two port network based behavioral model for dc-dc converter.

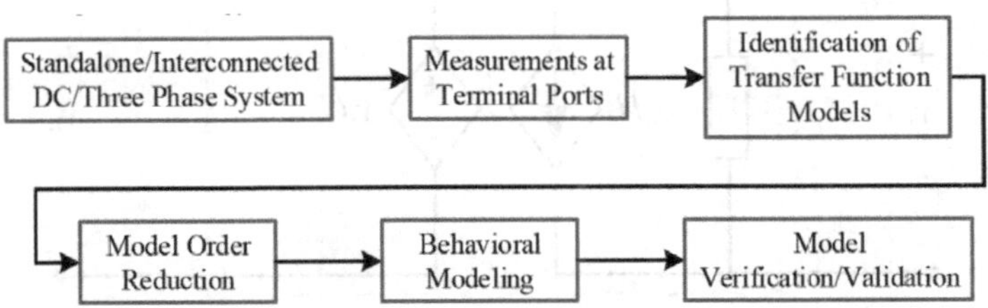

Figure 6.
General flowchart of behavioral modeling methodology.

commercial power electronics converters. The degree of matching between the results of actual system and its behavioral model is evaluated using root mean square deviation (RMSD). The two step, i.e. verification and validation based methodology serves well to authenticate the modeling procedure. **Figure 6** shows the general flowchart of behavioral modeling methodology.

6. Tow port network based behavioral modeling power electronic converters

Two port network based models have been extensively applied for the analysis of dc-dc converters [61, 62]. In the linear two port representation of dc-dc converters, the input and output port parameters constitute a set known as g-parameters. The un-terminated g-parameters represent the real internal dynamics excluding the source and load effects. The g-parameters based two port network model is used to build a small signal linear model of a dc-dc converter around a particular operating point. It is a hardware-oriented behavioral modeling approach, which does not require any prior information about either the topology or internal design of the converter. Hence there is no difference in the modeling methodology for various types of dc-dc converters, i.e., buck, boost, etc. The complete behavioral model is based upon the measurement and identification of four linear time invariant (LTI) models as transfer functions in the Laplace domain.

For the two-port network model shown in **Figure 7**, the input port is represented by a Norton equivalent circuit while the output port is represented by a Thevenin equivalent circuit [21]. It represents an un-terminated network, so the dynamic system based upon it results in a model which consists of the internal dynamics of the converter only. To achieve this the measurement setup should have minimum interaction either with the source or with the load. This is achieved when the converter is fed from a low output impedance voltage source and connected to an electronic load in constant current sink mode [63]. This setup helps in minimizing the effect of other elements such as filters and other converters upon the measurements for the system under test.

In **Figure** 7 the symbols can be generalized as v_j and i_j representing voltage and current, where $j \in (i, o)$, the subscripts i and o represent the input and output terminals respectively.

The four transfer functions shown in **Figure** 7, required to build the behavioral model are;

Y_i: Input admittance.

H_i: Back current gain.

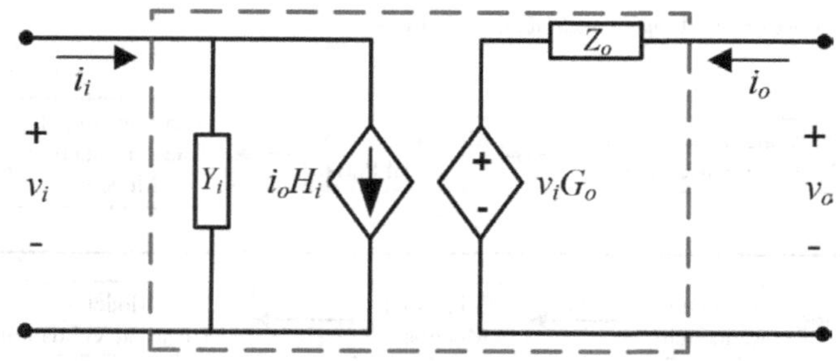

Figure 7.
G-parameters based two port network model for dc-dc converter.

G_o: Audiosusceptibility.
Z_o: Output impedance.
Mathematically the *g*-parameter set can be written as shown in Eq. (2)

$$Y_i = g_{11} = \left.\frac{i_i}{v_i}\right|_{i_o=0} \quad H_i = g_{12} = \left.\frac{i_i}{i_o}\right|_{v_i=0}$$
$$G_o = g_{21} = \left.\frac{v_o}{v_i}\right|_{i_o=0} \quad Z_o = g_{22} = \left.\frac{v_o}{i_o}\right|_{v_i=0} \tag{2}$$

In **Figure** 7, the direction of i_o shown results in a positive value for Z_o. In case the direction of i_o is reversed, then $(Z_o = -v_o/i_o)$ which will only result in phase shift of 180° for Z_o during the measurement.

The small signal input variables of the two port network are the input voltage and output current (v_i, i_o) while the small signal output variables are the output voltage and input current (v_o, i_i). In terms of these variables, the two port network model of **Figure** 7 can be represented in matrix form as shown in Eq. (3) [18].

$$\begin{bmatrix} i_i \\ v_o \end{bmatrix} = \begin{bmatrix} Y_i & H_i \\ G_o & Z_o \end{bmatrix} \begin{bmatrix} v_i \\ i_o \end{bmatrix} \tag{3}$$

The output impedance frequency response measurement contains information regarding the response of the converter to dynamic load changes at different frequencies. The output impedance shows how a converter regulates and responds to various load changes, while the input admittance does so concerning any interaction from the source. This determines the sensitivity of a power system to input filter or input power components. The input admittance measurement gives the designer idea about the integration of a power module into another system. An audiosusceptibility frequency response measurement determines the transmission of noise from the input of the system to the output. It tells about the ability of the converter to reject noise appearing at the input.

7. Conclusion

The focus of this chapter is to present a methodology for the development of behavioral models for various power electronics systems of more electric aircrafts. The dynamic behavioral models developed are being used to simulate, analyze and predict the behavior of the systems investigated. As most of the modern power electronics modules are black-box type, so the models representing these systems should be obtained via measurements at only the input–output terminals of the system. The resulting behavioral models should represent the internal dynamics of the system and predict its transient as well as steady state behavior. Thus the proposed behavioral modeling methodology can be successfully applied to standalone power electronic converters as well as complex systems comprising of multiple sources, interface converters and loads. The model verification is done by application of certain test signals to the actual system and its behavioral models and then comparing the response of both. The close matching of results would confirm the accurate modeling.

References

[1] Roque PMJ, Chowdhury SP, and Huan Z. The role of microgrids on decoupling sharp fluctuations of electricity demand in centralized power System. In Proceedings of the 51st International Universities Power Eng ineering Conference (UPEC); 6-9 Sept. 2016; Portugal.

[2] Sherpa L, Urundady V, Rai B. Hybrid PV/wind energy system with a centralized dc bus architecture and power regulation. In Proceedings of the Annual IEEE India Conference (INDICON); 17-20 Dec. 2015; India; p. 1-6 .

[3] Miftakhutdinov R. Power distribution architecture for tele- and data communication system based on new generation intermediate bus converter. In Proceedings of the IEEE 30th International Telecommunications Energy Conference (INTELEC); 14-18 Sept. 2008; USA; p. 1-8.

[4] Emadi A. Modeling and analysis of multiconverter dc power electronic systems using the generalized state-space averaging method. IEEE Transactions on Industrial Electronics. June 2004; vol. 51, no. 3, 661-668.

[5] Sanz M, Bermejo M, Lazaro A, Lopez-del-Moral D, Zumel P, Fernandez C, Barrado A. Simple input impedance converter model to design regulators for dc-distributed system. In Proceedings of the IEEE 17th Workshop on Control and Modeling for Power Electronics (COMPEL); 27-30 June 2016; Norway.

[6] Gerber JP, Oliver JA, Cordero N, Harder T, Cobos JA, Hayes M, O'Mathuna SC, Prem E. Power electronics enabling efficient energy usage: Energy savings potential and technological challenges. IEEE Transactions on Power Electronics. May 2012; vol. 27, no. 5, 2338-2353.

[7] Boroyevich D, Cvetkovic I, Dong D, Burgos R, Fei W, Lee F. Future electronic power distribution systems a contemplative view. In Proceedings of the 12th International Conference on Optimization of Electrical and Electronic Equipment (OPTIM); 20-22 May 2010; p. 1369-1380.

[8] Dragicevic T, Vasquez JC, Guerrero JM, and Skrlec D. Advanced LVDC electrical power architectures and microgrids: A step toward a new generation of power distribution networks. IEEE Electrification Magazine. March 2014; vol. 2, 54–65.

[9] Lam E, Bell R, Ashley D. Revolutionary advances in distributed power systems. In Proceedings of the 18th Annual IEEE Applied Power Electronics Conference and Exposition (APEC '03); 9-13 Feb. 2003; p.30-36.

[10] Hayashi Y. Approach for highly efficient and ultra compact converters in next generation 380 V DC distribution system. In Proceedings of the IEEE Energy Conversion Congress and Exposition (ECCE); 15-20 Sept. 2012; USA; p. 3803-3810.

[11] Sarlioglu B, Morris CT. More electric aircraft: Review, challenges, and opportunities for commercial transport aircraft. IEEE Transactions on Transportation Electrification. June 2015; vol. 1, no. 1, 54-56.

[12] Jayabalan R, Fahimi B, Koenig A, Pekarek S. Applications of power electronics-based systems in vehicular technology: State-of-the art and future trends. In Proceedings of the 35th Annual IEEE Power Electronics Specialists Conference (PESC '04); 20-25 June 2004; Germany; p.1887-1894

[13] Ouroua A, Domaschk L, Beno JH. Electric ship power system integration analyses through modeling and

simulation. In Proceedings of the IEEE Electric Ship Technologies Symposium; 27 July 2005; USA; p. 70-74.

[14] Schulz W. ETSI standards and guides for efficient powering of telecommunication and datacom. In Proceedings of the 29th International Telecommunications Energy Conference (INTELEC); 30 Sept.-4 Oct. 2007; Italy; p. 168-173.

[15] Boroyevich D, Cvetkovic I, Burgos R, Dong D. Intergrid: A future electronic energy network. IEEE Journal of Emerging and Selected Topics in Power Electronics, Sept. 2013; vol. 1, no. 3.

[16] Wu TF, Chen YK, Yu GR, Chang YC. Design and development of dc-distributed system with grid connection for residential applications. In Proceedings of the IEEE 8th International Conference on Power Electronics and ECCE Asia (ICPE& ECCE); 30 May-3 June 2011; Korea; p. 235-241.

[17] Sanz M, Valdivia V, Zumel P, Moral DL, Fernández C, Lázaro L, Barrado A. Analysis of the Stability of Power Electronics Systems: A Practical Approach. In Proceedings of the 29th Annual IEEE Applied Power Electronics Conference and Exposition (APEC); 16-20 March 2014; USA; p. 2682-2689.

[18] Cho BH, Lee FC. Modeling and analysis of spacecraft power systems. IEEE Transactions on Power Electronics. Jan. 1988; vol. 3, no. 1, 44-54.

[19] Kwon JB, Wang X, Blaabjerg F, Bak CL. Frequency-domain modeling and simulation of dc power electronic systems using harmonic state space method. IEEE Transactions on Power Electronics. vol. 32, no. 2, 1044-1055.

[20] Oliver JA, Prieto R, Laguna L, Cobos JA. Modeling and simulation requirements for the analysis and design of dc distributed power electronic systems. In Proceedings of the 11th IEEE International Power Electronics Congress; 24-27 Aug. 2008; Mexico; p. 204-209.

[21] Arnedo L, Burgos R, Wang F, Boroyevich D. Black-box terminal characterization modeling of DC to DC Converters. In Proceedings of the 22nd Annual IEEE Applied Power Electronics Conference and Exposition (APEC'07); 25 Feb.-1 March 2007; USA; p. 457-463.

[22] Ortiz CEC. Circuit oriented average modeling of switching power converters. In Proceedings of the 2005 European Conference on Power Electronics and Applications; 11-14 Sept. 2005; Germany; p.P.1-P.10

[23] Sun J. Characterization and performance comparison of ripple-based control for voltage regulator modules. IEEE Transactions on Power Electronics. March 2006; vol. 21, no. 2, 346-353.

[24] Available from: Vicor, V24C5C100BL, http://cdn.vicorpower.com/documents/datasheets/ds_24vin-micro-family.pdf, 2016. [Accessed: 2020-06-20]

[25] Rubino L, Iannuzzi D, Rubino G, Coppola M, Marino P. Concept of energy management for advanced smart-grid power distribution system in aeronautical applications. In Proceedings of the International Conference on Electrical Systems for Aircraft, Railway, Ship Propulsion and Road Vehicles & International Transportation Electrification Conference (ESARS-ITEC), 2-4 Nov. 2016; France.

[26] Sun J. AC power electronics systems: stability and power quality. In Proceedings of the 11th Workshop on Control and Modeling; 17-20 Aug. 2008; Switzerland; p. 1-10.

[27] Chiniforoosh S, Jatskevich J, Yazdani A, Sood V, Dinavahi V, Martinez JA, Ramirez A. Definitions and applications of dynamic average models for analysis of power systems. IEEE Transactions on Power Delivery. Oct. 2010; vol. 25. no. 4, 2655-2669.

[28] Mocci A, Serpi A, Marongiu I, Gatto G. Enhanced modeling of dc-dc power converters by means of averaging technique. In Proceedings of the 40th Annual Conference of the IEEE Industrial Electronics Society (IECON); 29 Oct.-1 Nov. 2014, USA, p. 5101-5107.

[29] Erickson RW, Maksimovic D. Fundamentals of Power Electronics, 2nd Ed., Springer, Jan. 2001.

[30] Baisden AC, Boroyevich D, Wyk JDV. Impedance interaction and EMI attenuation in converters with an integrated transmission-line filter. In Proceedings of the 22nd Annual IEEE Applied Power Electronics Conference and Exposition; 25 Feb.-1 March 2007; USA; p.1203-1208.

[31] Wester GW, Middlebrook RD. Low-frequency characterization of switched dc-dc converters. IEEE Transactions on Aerospace and Electronic Systems. May 1973; vol. AES-9, no. 3, 376-385.

[32] Sanders SR, Noworolski JM, Liu XZ, Verghese GC. Generalized averaging method for power conversion circuits. IEEE Transactions on Power Electronics. Apr 1991, vol. 6, no. 2, 251-259.

[33] Shortt DG, Lee FC. Improved switching converter model using discrete and averaging techniques. IEEE Transactions on Aerospace and Electronic Systems, March 1983; vol. AES-19, no. 2, pp. 190-202.

[34] Foster MP, Sewell HI, Bingham CM, Stone DA, Hente D, Howe D. Cyclic-averaging for high-speed analysis of resonant converters. IEEE Transactions on Power Electronics. July 2003; vol. 18, no. 4, 985-993.

[35] Hiti S, Boroyevich D, Cuadros C. Small-signal modeling and control of three-phase PWM converters. In Proceedings of the IEEE Industrial Applications Society Annual Meeting; 2-6 Oct. 1994; USA; p.1143-1150.

[36] Jaksic M, Shen Z, Cvetkovic I, Boroyevich D, Burgos R. Analysis of nonlinear sideband effects in small-signal input dq admittance of twelve-pulse diode rectifiers. In Proceedings of IEEE Energy Conversion Congress and Exposition (ECCE); 15-19 Sept. 2013; USA; p. 3356-3362

[37] Chiniforoosh S, Atighechi H, Jatskevich J. A generalized methodology for dynamic average modeling of high-pulse-count rectifiers in transient simulation programs. IEEE Transactions on Energy Conversion. Mar. 2016; vol. 31, no. 1, 228-239.

[38] Aguirre LA, Garcia PGD, Filho RS. Use of a priori information in the identification of global nonlinear models-a case study using a buck converter. IEEE Transactions on Circuits and Systems I: Fundamental Theory and Applications. July 2000. vol. 47, no. 7, 1081-1085.

[39] Prieto R, Ruiz LL, Oliver JA, Cobos JA. Parameterization of dc/dc converter models for system level simulation. In Proceedings of the European Conference on Power Electronics and Applications; 2-5 Sept. 2007; Denmark; p. 1-10.

[40] Oliver JA, Prieto R, Romero V, Cobos JA. Behavioral modeling of dc-dc converters for large-signal simulation of distributed power systems. In Proceedings of the 21st Annual IEEE Applied Power Electronics Conference and Exposition (APEC'06); 19-23 March 2006; USA.

[41] Middlebrook RD. Measurement of loop gain in feedback systems. International Journal of Electronics, pp. 485-512, vol. 38, no. 4, 1975.

[42] Huynh P, Cho BH. Empirical small-signal modeling of switching converters using Pspice. In Proceedings of 26th Annual IEEE Power Electronics Specialists Conference (PESC), 18-22 June 1995; p. 809-815.

[43] Maksimovic D. Computer-aided small-signal analysis based on impulse response of dc/dc switching power converters. IEEE Transactions on Power Electronics. Nov. 2000; vol. 15, no. 6, 1183-1191.

[44] Barkley A. Santi E. Improved online identification of a dc–dc converter and its control loop gain using cross-correlation methods. IEEE Transactions on Power Electronics. Aug. 2009; vol. 24, no. 8, 2021-2031.

[45] Yeop CJ, Cho BH, Landingham HFV, Soo MH, Ho SJ. System identification of power converters based on a black-box approach. IEEE Transactions on Circuits and Systems I. Nov. 1998; vol. 45, no. 11, 1148-1158.

[46] Lee JR, Cho BH, Kim SJ, Lee FC. Modeling and simulation of spacecraft power systems. IEEE Transactions on Aerospace and Electronic Systems. May 1988; vol. 24, no. 3, 295-304.

[47] Chau KT, Chan CC. Nonlinear identification of power electronic systems. In Proceedings of The International Conference on Power Electronics and Drive Systems; 21-24 Feb. 1995; p. 329-334, Singapore.

[48] Leyva R, Salamero LM, Jammes B, Marpinard JC, Guinjoan F. Identification and control of power converters by means of neural networks. IEEE Transactions on Circuits and Systems. Aug. 1997; vol. 44, no. 8, 735-742.

[49] Oliver JA, Prieto R, Cobos JA, Garcia O, Alou P. Hybrid Wiener-Hammerstein structure for grey-box modeling of dc-dc converters. In Proceedings of the 24th Annual IEEE Applied Power Electronics Conference and Exposition (APEC); 15-19 Feb. 2009; USA; p. 280-285.

[50] Alonge F, Rabbeni R, Pucci M, Vitale G. Identification and robust control of a quadratic dc/dc boost converter by Hammerstein model. IEEE Transactions on Industry Applications. Sept./Oct. 2015; vol. 51, no. 5, 3975-3985.

[51] Maranesi PG, Tavazzi V, Varoli V. Two-port characterization of PWM voltage regulators at low frequencies. IEEE Transactions on Industrial Electronics. Aug. 1988; vol. 35, no. 3, 444-450.

[52] Suntio T, Gadoura D. Use of unterminated two-port modeling technique in analysis of input filter interactions in telecom DPS systems. In Proceedings of the 24th Annual International Telecommunications Energy Conference; 29 Sept.-3 Oct. 2002; p.560-565.

[53] Cvetkovic I, Boroyevich D, Mattavelli P, Lee FC, Dong D. Nonlinear, hybrid terminal behavioral modeling of a dc-based nanogrid system. In Proceedings of the 26th Annual IEEE Applied Power Electronics Conference and Exposition (APEC); 6-11 March 2011; USA; p. 1251-1258.

[54] Frances, A, Asensi R, Garcia O, Prieto, R, Uceda J. How to model a DC microgrid: towards an automated solution. In Proceedings of the IEEE 2nd International Conference on DC Microgrids (ICDCM); 27–29 June 2017; Nuremburg, Germany.

[55] Shi Y, Xu D, Su J, Liu N, Yu H, Xu H. Black-Box Behavioral Modeling of Voltage and Frequency Response Characteristic for Islanded Microgrid. Energies. 2019.

[56] Frances A, Asensi R, García O, Prieto R, Uceda J. Modeling Electronic Power Converters in Smart DC Microgrids – An Overview. IEEE Transactions on Smart Grid. 2020.

[57] Francés A, Asensi R, García O, Uceda J. A blackbox large signal Lyapunov-based stability analysis method for power converter-based systems. In Proceedings of the IEEE 17th Workshop on Control and Modeling for Power Electronics (COMPEL); 27–30 June 2016; Trondheim, Norway; p. 1–6.

[58] Cvetkovic I, Boroyevich D, Burgos R, Liu Z. Generalized Behavioral Models of Three-Phase Converters and Electric Machines for System-Level Study and Stability Assessment. In Proceedings of IEEE International Symposium on Power Electronics for Distributed Generation Systems (PEDG); 28 Sept.-1Oct. 2020; Croatia.

[59] Available from: MathWorks: http://www.mathworks.com. [Accessed: 2020-06-25]

[60] Available from: https://www.synopsys.com/verification/virtual-prototyping/saber.html [Accessed: 2020-06-30]

[61] Roinila T, Hankaniemi M, Suntio T, Sippola M, Vilkko M. Dynamical profile of a switched-mode converter – Reality or imagination. In Proceedings of the 29th International Telecommunications Energy Conference (INTELEC); 30 Sept.-4 Oct. 2007; pp. 420-427.

[62] Suntio T. Unified average and small-signal modeling of direct-on-time control. IEEE Transactions on Industrial Electronics. Feb. 2006; vol. 53, no. 1, 287-295.

[63] Arnedo L, Boroyevich D, Burgos R, Wang F. Un-terminated frequency response measurements and model order reduction for black box terminal characterization models. In Proceedings of the 23rd Annual IEEE Applied Power Electronics Conference and Exposition (APEC); 24-28 Feb. 2008; USA: p. 1054-1060.

Chapter 5

Online Estimation of Terminal Airspace Sector Capacity from ATC Workload

Abstract

Neural Partial Differentiation (NPD) approach is applied to estimate terminal airspace sector capacity in real-time from the ATC (Air Traffic Controller) dynamical neural model with permissible safe separation and affordable workload. A neural model of a multi-input-single-output (MISO) ATC dynamical system is primarily established and used to estimate parameters from the experimental data using NPD. Since the relative standard deviations of these estimated parameters are lesser, the predicted neural model response is well matched with the intervention of ATC workload. Moreover, the proposed neural network-based approach works well with the experimental data online as it does not require the initial values of model parameters that are unknown in practice.

Keywords: ATC (Air Traffic Controller) workload, terminal airspace capacity, estimation and dynamic modeling, neural partial differentiation, output error method

1. Introduction

Accurate estimation of the air traffic capacity is a pillar of efficient air traffic management, which provide efficient use of airspace resources and controlling resources to meet the air traffic demand [1]. Suppose trajectories of all flights and the capacity of all resources are known with certainty for some planning horizon. In that case, there exist computationally feasible approaches to managing the traffic that minimizes overall delay cost [2–6]. But the uncertainty makes traffic flow management difficult. At any given time, the weather is the driving force in determining the number of flights in the airport or sector in the aspect of capacity. Air traffic controllers (ATC) confirm airspace's safe operation by ensuring all aircraft under their authority maintain safe separation with the assistance of technology and international rules and regulations [7]. The role of ATC is becoming more crucial as air traffic growth increases. So traffic growth will introduce more aircraft operations in the busy ATC sectors with high air traffic density. The significant effect of such an increase in air traffic has been the rise in flight delays in the region. As a result, an economic impact of flight delays is included in the safe operation of airspace. Individual aircraft delay is increased whenever air traffic demand nears capacity. Therefore, unacceptable delays result from exceeding progressive hourly traffic demands to the hourly capacity of the air traffic. The aircraft delays will not decrease even if the hourly demand is less than the hourly capacity for the demand within a portion of the time interval that exceeds the capacity during that interval.

In the en-route environment, the airspace is segmented into air traffic control ATC sectors, the geographical volume of airspace. By keeping safety as a priority in operation, the capacity of an ATC sector can be defined as the maximum number of aircraft that are controlled in a particular ATC sector in a specified period while still permitting an acceptable level of controller workload. For more clarity, we need to realize i) What is meant by the controller workload? ii) How is this controller workload measured? iii) What is the acceptable level of controller workload? i.e. the threshold value at capacity. Thus, the workload is a process or experience that cannot be seen directly but must be understood from what can be seen or measured. In the present scenario of air transport, air traffic is increasing rapidly and becomes airspace congestion. Airspace capacity needs to be increased to address the airspace congestion problem. Since the airspace sector capacity is determined mainly by controller workload, a typical air transport schematic is given in **Figure 1**, highlighting the controller workload problem [8, 9]. Controller workload is the effort expended by the controller to manage air traffic events. It refers to the physical and mental effort an individual exerts to perform a task. A measure of the ATC Workload is required to evaluate the effects of new systems and the procedures on individual air traffic controllers.

Certain airspace capacity issues can be addressed by minimizing the controller overload and clarifying the necessity of understanding and modeling the controller workload. The critical factors affecting controller workload are sector, and air traffic characteristics [8, 9] and those factors are given in **Figure 2**. The factors affecting air traffic and sectors are listed in **Table 1** [10]. Measurement of controller workload can be achieved from the information on the i) communication between the ATC officer and the pilot and ii) communication between the ATC officers of adjacent sectors. The number of aircraft movements per hour, number of heading changes, number of altitudes changes and number of speed changes are the information on monitoring workload. Various methods are discussed in the literature for measuring the workload of air traffic controllers [11, 12]. They are self-assessment [13, 14] and direct observations of the controllers by other controllers or ATC system experts. Moreover, the workload experienced by air traffic controllers is affected by the complex integration of: 1) the air traffic and the sector in the airspace, 2) the accuracy of equipment in the control room and in the aircraft, and 3) the controller's

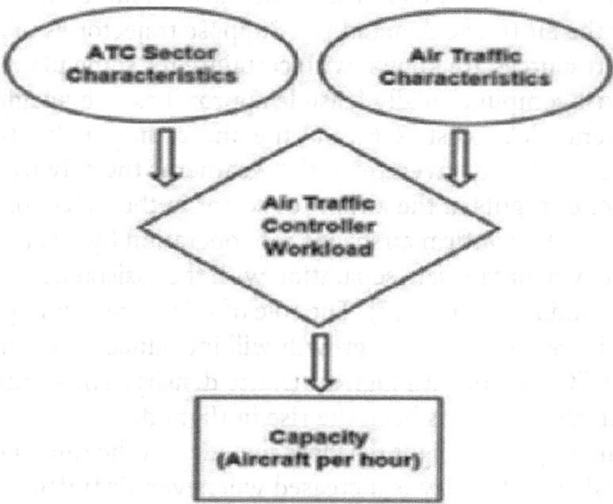

Figure 1.
Air transport schematic with controller workload.

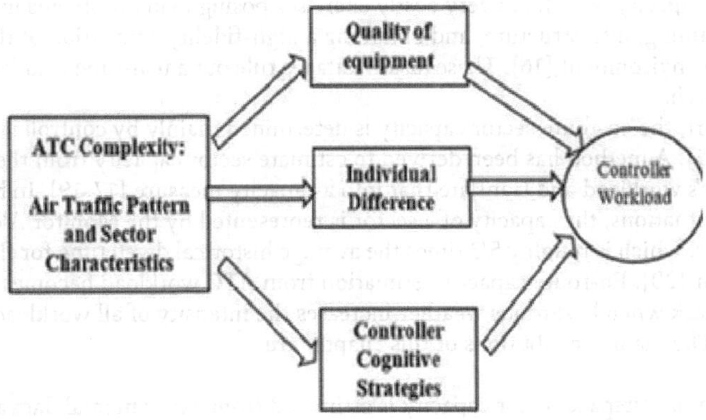

Figure 2.
Controller workload factors.

Sr. No	Factors affecting air traffic	Factors affecting sectors
1	Total number of aircraft	Sector size
2	Peak hourly count	Sector shape
3	Traffic Mix	Boundary location
4	Climbing / Descending aircraft	Number of intersection points
5	Aircraft speeds	Number of flight levels
6	Horizontal separation standards	Number of facilities
7	Vertical separation standards	Number of entry and exit points
8	Average flight duration in sector	Airway Configuration
9	Total flight time in sector	Proportion of unidirectional routes
10	Average flight direction	Number of surrounding sectors

Table 1.
Factors affecting air traffic and sector.

age, experience, decision-making strategies. Another possible approach to measuring ATC workload is to form a functional relationship between the controller workload and the associated model parameters. To achieve that relationship, we must vary several possible airspace and traffic parameters systematically in simulation modeling of airspace and controller workload [15].

The ideal approach to estimate airspace capacity is to build an accurate capacity model from the direct observation of the controller's workload using a system identification procedure. The derived statistical model will represent the actual capacity of sectors and airspace under alternative controller working processes [8]. To validate such a model, one needs to collect the data for a sufficient period and over a range of different individual controllers. Many difficulties need to address the collection of field data at each ATC sector. Observing controllers at work as unobtrusively as possible is not an easy task. Moreover, more resources are also required to transcribe the data from videotape, communications tapes, and flight strips. As a result, vast resources and complex logistics are needed for this approach precluded for this research. The construction of an operational environment using real-time simulations is an alternative method with the technology to be tested and pseudo-pilots. Such real-time simulation provides the human workload and traffic handling capacity, which are very costly exercises posing many problems in personnel training, infrastructure, and obtaining a high-fidelity simulation of the operating environment [16]. These disadvantages rule out a real-time simulation for this research.

In short, the en-route sector capacity is determined mainly by controller workload [9, 17]. A method has been derived to estimate sector capacity from the controller's workload and translate that into a capacity measure [17–19]. In bright weather situations, the capacity of a sector is represented by the Monitor Alert Parameter, which is roughly 5/3 times the average historical dwell time for flights in that sector [20]. En-route capacity estimation from ATC workload becomes a more difficult task when hazardous weather increases the intensity of all workload types [21–23]. The main contributions of this chapter are

- Terminal airspace sector capacity is estimated from experimental data along with the derivation of ATC dynamical model. Neural partial differentiation (NPD) and output error method (OEM) are used for this purpose, and their results are compared. An appropriate probability density function (pdf) of'Time interval X' is derived and analytically verified for the accurate modeling of ATC dynamic system.

- Since the uncertainty in traffic flow and dependency of weather conditions make the data to stochastic, the proposed neural network-based approach works well with the experimental data in online as it can handle the noisy data without knowing the noise covariance matrix and does not require the initial values of the model parameters which are unknown in practice. As a result, a three-dimensional capacity curve has been established using the estimates of NPD to predict the air traffic capacity in real-time.

The chapter is organized as follows: Section 2 discusses mathematical model postulates for the estimation of Terminal Airspace Capacity with analysis of flight data. Moreover, dynamic modeling of ATC with estimation of model parameters using neural partial differentiation (NPD) are described in the following subsections of section 2. The online estimation result of airspace capacity is presented in Section 3, and finally, the conclusions are given in Section 4.

2. Estimation of terminal airspace sector capacity

2.1 Problem definition

The estimation of airspace sector capacity $C_s(k)$ in (Eq.(1)) can be viewed as dynamic modeling of ATC by estimating the parameter θ at which variables x_1, x_2, x_3 are satisfying the following inequality relation (Eq.(2)) with maximum affordable value of ATC workload represented in terms of $G(.)$;

$$C_s(k) = x_1(k) + x_2(k) + x_3(k) \tag{1}$$

$$f(x_1(k), x_2(k), x_3(k), \theta) \le G(h(X(k))), k = 1, 2, 3, \ldots, N \tag{2}$$

where $f(x_1, x_2, x_3, \theta)$ represents the dynamical model of ATC, θ is the vector of model parameters, x_1 is total number of departing aircraft during an unit time, x_2 is total number of arriving aircraft during an unit time, x_3 is total number of flyover aircraft during an unit time, $G(.)$ is number of control events (messages between pilot and ATC) that occurred in unit time, h(X) is function associated with the workload of ATC, and X is interval time of the consecutive events (messages) in sec.

2.2 Flight data analysis

The recorded flight data of the third sector of Kunming TMA at Kunming airport, China is analyzed to estimate the terminal airspace sector capacity from the ATC workload [24]. Terminal Maneuvering Area (TMA) is designated area of controlled airspace surrounding a significant airport where there is a high volume of traffic. This data is based on the workload of ATC during the entire day; it consists of voice communication (messages) between ATC officers and pilots or adjacent sectors. These messages are referred to control events exhibit intermittency, i.e., they occur in several time frames with "short interval and high frequency" or vice versa based on the traffic congestion. For the definition of a function h(X) in (Eq.(2), the field data of air traffic can be gathered from the ATC officers at the Kunming airport using voice recording equipment of the air traffic control department. The time interval of the 1000 consecutive events on 21st January 2014, is recorded in the third sector of Kunming TMA, which is given in **Figure 3** [24].

Data statistics are made with MATLAB and found the histogram of time interval X to derive the density distribution function $P(X)$ in **Figure 4**. This indicates that experimental data show power-law distribution whose probability density function is given by.

$$P(X) = CX^{-\alpha} \tag{3}$$

The distribution characteristics of power-law function can be verified by a theoretical method; the parameter C and α are computed by the following maximum likelihood estimation (MLE) approach. By taking the logarithm of (Eq.(3)), we have.

$$\log(P(X)) = \log(C) - \alpha \log(X) \tag{4}$$

The relationship represents a straight line with a gradient of $-\alpha$ in the double logarithmic coordinates. The normalization equation is.

$$1 = \int_{X_{\min}}^{\infty} P(X)dX = C \int_{X_{\min}}^{\infty} X^{-\alpha}dX \Rightarrow C = (\alpha - 1)X_{\min}^{\alpha-1}, \alpha > 1 \tag{5}$$

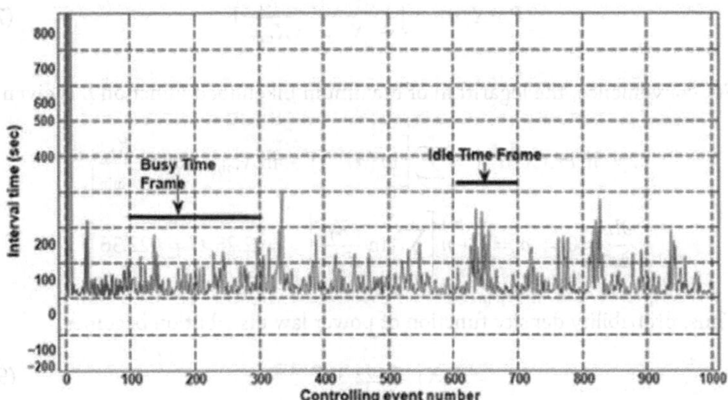

Figure 3.
Interval time of ATC.

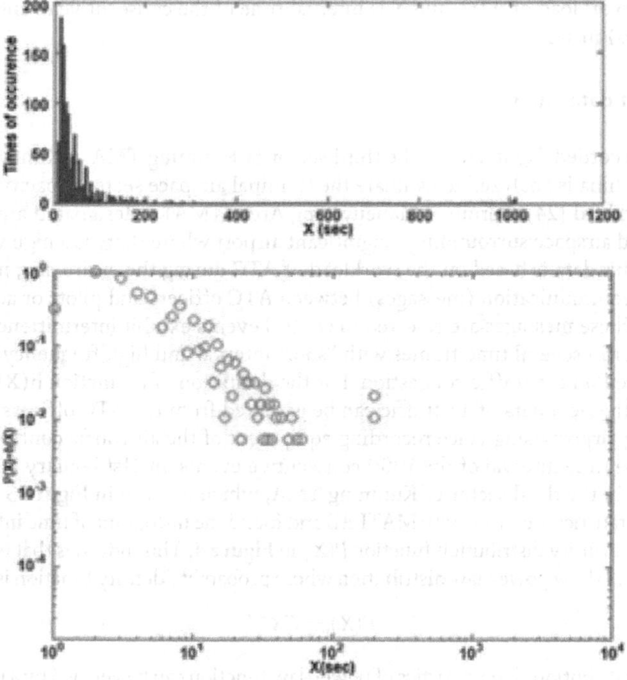

Figure 4.
Density distribution of Time Interval.

Where X_{min} is the minimum possible value of X. The power law distribution is

$$P(X) = \frac{(\alpha - 1)}{X_{\min}} \left(\frac{X}{X_{\min}} \right)^{-\alpha} \tag{6}$$

For a given set X_i, probability of X_i is

$$Pr.(X/\alpha) = \prod_{i=1}^{N} \frac{(\alpha - 1)}{X_{\min}} \left(\frac{X_i}{X_{\min}} \right)^{-\alpha} \tag{7}$$

For convenience, the logarithm of Maximum Likelihood Function L is given by

$$\begin{aligned} L = \ln Pr.(X/\alpha\ ) &= \sum_{i=1}^{n} \left[\ln(\alpha - 1) - \ln X_{\min} - \alpha \ln \frac{X_i}{X_{\min}} \right] \\ \frac{\partial L}{\partial \alpha} = 0 \Rightarrow \alpha &= 1 + n \left[\sum_{i=1}^{n} \ln \frac{X_i}{X_{\min}} \right]^{-1} = 2.25, C = 122.36 \end{aligned} \tag{8}$$

Thus, probability density function of power law distribution becomes.

$$P(X) = 122.36X^{-2.25} \tag{9}$$

We found that the experimental data agree with the distribution characteristic of power-law function by theoretical computation of (Eq.(9)) as shown in **Figure 5**.

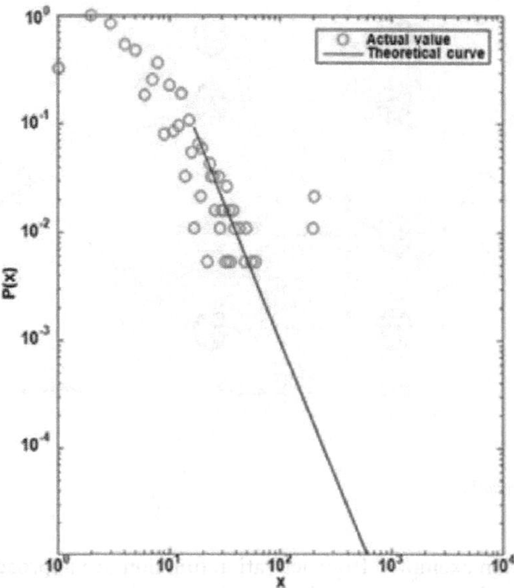

Figure 5.
Density distribution of Time Interval.

The R^2 value of the data fitting is observed to be 0.83. Now the left side of expression $G(h(X))$ in (Eq.(2)) can be computed with the threshold criterion of 80 percent. Since the sector capacity is expressed in terms of a number of control events that occurred within one hour of the estimation time, the reasonable controlling workload time should be $2880(= 3600 * 80/100)$ seconds. Subsequently, sector capacity is estimated by representing $G(h(X))$ is the number of control events that occurred within one hour as follows.

$$G(.) = \frac{2880}{E(X)} \tag{10}$$

where $E(X)$ is average interval time (X) of the consecutive events in sec, and it is given by

$$E(X) = \left(\frac{C}{\alpha - 1}\right)^{\frac{1}{\alpha-1}} \left(\frac{\alpha - 2}{\alpha - 1}\right), \alpha > 2 \tag{11}$$

Next, to estimate the airspace sector capacity, we need to build the dynamical model of ATC and estimate the model parameters.

2.3 ATC dynamic modeling and parameter estimation

2.3.1 Neural dynamic modeling of ATC

Based on the equality relation of (Eq.(1)), the dynamical model of ATC represented by $f(x_1, x_2, x_3, \theta)$ can be modeled using Neural Networks [25]. **Figure 6** shows the three-layered feed-forward neural network's schematic structure, which consists of two hidden layers with activation function and one output layer with

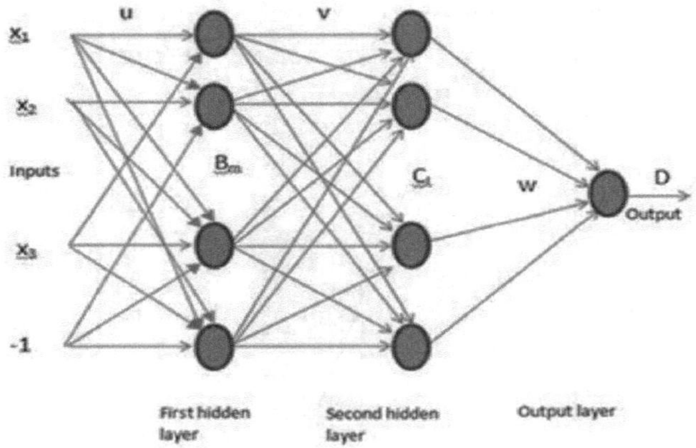

Figure 6.
Schematic of neural network.

summation function exempted from activation function. An approach of back-propagation trains the neural network whose input and output vectors are defined by $x = [x_1, x_2, x_3, -1]$ and $D = G$ respectively. Similarly, $B \in \Re^{m+1}$ and $C \in \Re^{l+1}$ represents the first and second hidden layer of neural network. Except for the output layer, all the layers contain a bias term, and the output of the neural network is given by.

$$G = W^T C \tag{12}$$

where W is the set of weights between the second hidden layer and output layer containing the bias terms.

$$W = [b_{w1} \quad w_{11} \quad \cdots \quad w_{l1}]^T \tag{13}$$

Similarly we define

$$\begin{cases} C = q(V^T B) \\ B = g(U^T x) \end{cases} \tag{14}$$

where q and g are the activation function vectors and are defined as $[-1\, q(x_1)]^T$, where $q(x)$ is expressed as

$$q(x) = \frac{1 - e^{-\lambda x}}{1 + e^{-\lambda x}} \tag{15}$$

And the weight matrix are represented as

$$[V] = \begin{bmatrix} b_{v1} & \dots & b_{vm} \\ v_{11} & \dots & v_{1l} \\ \dots & \dots & \dots \\ v_{m1} & \dots & v_{ml} \end{bmatrix} \tag{16}$$

$$[U] = \begin{bmatrix} b_{u1} & \dots & b_{um} \\ u_{11} & \dots & u_{1m} \\ u_{21} & \dots & u_{2m} \\ u_{31} & \dots & u_{3m} \end{bmatrix} \tag{17}$$

Input is defined by the vector $x = [x_0, x_1, x_2, x_3]$, where x_0 defines bias input to the neural network. The input and output are scaled for neural network using the following equation.

$$G_{i,norm} = G_{i,norm_{\min}} + (G_{i,norm_{\max}} - G_{i,norm_{\min}}) \times \left(\frac{G_i - G_{i,\min}}{G_{i,\max} - G_{i,\min}} \right) \tag{18}$$

where $G_{i,norm_{\max}}$ and $G_{i,norm_{\min}}$ denote the higher and lower limits of scaling range of G_i respectively. They are set to 0.9 and $-$ 0.9 respectively. $G_{i,max}$ and $G_{i,\min}$ denote the higher and lower values of G_i. Using the above notations, output of neural network can be written as.

$$G = W^T q\left[V^T g(U^T x)\right] \tag{19}$$

2.3.2 Parameter estimation using neural partial differentiation method

The neural network is trained with input and output data to map the functional relationship of (Eq.(1)) in the form of weights, and its activation function operates the core of the neural partial differentiation method as parameter estimation approach. The constant parameters of air traffic model can be directly computed from the end of the training session of a neural network by the partial differentiation of a function, and it is as follows.

The input and output of a function is mapped after the training session of the neural network. Subsequently, the output variables can be differentiated with respect to input variables. Differentiate (Eq.(12)) and (Eq.(14)), we will have the form of.

$$\frac{\partial G}{\partial C} = W^T \tag{20}$$

$$\frac{\partial C}{\partial B} = q'\left(V^T\right) \tag{21}$$

$$\frac{\partial B}{\partial x} = g'\left(U^T\right) \tag{22}$$

Multiplication of (Eq.(20)), (Eq.(21))), and (Eq.(22)) gives.

$$\begin{cases} \dfrac{\partial G}{\partial C} \cdot \dfrac{\partial C}{\partial B} \cdot \dfrac{\partial B}{\partial x} = W^T . q' V^T . g' U^T \\ \dfrac{\partial G}{\partial x} = W^T . q' V^T . g' U^T \end{cases} \tag{23}$$

where $q' = diag\left[0\ q'_1 \cdots q'_l\right]$ and $g' = diag\left[0\ g'_1 \quad \cdots \quad g'_m\right]$. If the input and output of neural network are normalized, then

$$\frac{\partial G}{\partial x} = \frac{\partial G}{\partial G_{norm}} \times \frac{\partial G_{norm}}{\partial x_{norm}} \times \frac{\partial x_{norm}}{\partial x} \tag{24}$$

The normalized output of neural network can be de-normalized by (Eq.(18)). Where,

$$\left[\frac{\partial x_{norm}}{\partial x}\right] = \begin{bmatrix} 1 & 0 & 0 & 0 \\ 0 & \frac{\partial x_{1,norm}}{\partial x_1} & 0 & 0 \\ 0 & 0 & \frac{\partial x_{2,norm}}{\partial x_2} & 0 \\ 0 & 0 & 0 & \frac{\partial x_{3,norm}}{\partial x_3} \end{bmatrix} \tag{25}$$

The equation (Eq.(25)) can be computed from (Eq.(18)). The terms associated of (Eq.(20)) to (Eq.(25)) be intermediate terms of neural networks while getting it trained. Therefore, there is no extra computation required to compute the parameters, and they are directly given as:

$$\left\{\frac{\partial G}{\partial x}\right\} = \left[\frac{\partial G}{\partial x_0} \quad \frac{\partial G}{\partial x_1} \quad \frac{\partial G}{\partial x_2} \quad \frac{\partial G}{\partial x_3}\right] \tag{26}$$

The standard deviation of estimated parameters in (Eq.(26)) is computed by

$$S_{TD} = \sqrt{\frac{\sum_{p=1}^{P}\left[\sum_{m=1}^{M}\left(\sum_{l=1}^{L} C'_{l_p} v_{lm} w_{kl} G'_{k_p}\right) B'_{m_p} u_{mi} - \mu\right]^2}{P}} \tag{27}$$

where,

$$\mu = \frac{\sum_{p=1}^{P}\sum_{m=1}^{M}\left(\sum_{l=1}^{L} C'_{l_p} v_{lm} w_{kl} G'_{k_p}\right) B'_{m_p} u_{mi}}{P} \tag{28}$$

where, S_{TD} and μ are standard deviation and average of data points, respectively. The relative standard deviation of estimates is given by

$$R_{STD} = \frac{S_{TD}}{\mu} \times 100\% \tag{29}$$

3. Online estimation results and discussion

As a part of ATC dynamic modeling, online estimation of the model parameters from flight data is carried out using Neural partial differentiation (NPD) method [26], and estimates are compared with that obtained by Maximum likelihood estimation (Output Error Method). The model structure of the dynamical ATC is given by [27].

$$y = x_1\beta_1 + x_2\beta_2 + x_3\beta_3 + e \tag{30}$$

where y is the number of control events that occurred in unit time, which represents an ATC workload, x_1 is the total number of arriving aircraft during a unit time, x_2 is the total number of departing aircraft during a unit time, x_3 is the total number of flyover aircraft during a unit time. ATC model parameters $\beta_1, \beta_2, \beta_3$ in (Eq.(30)) are coefficient terms which are needed to be estimated for a given set of y and x_1, x_2, x_3 values, and e is a random error term represents model uncertainty. A neural model of ATC has been established by training of the input–output flight data. An approach of Neural Partial Differentiation (NPD) can be applied to extract the model parameters $\beta_1, \beta_2, \beta_3$. From the neural model of ATC, and their corresponding standard and relative standard deviations can compute using (Eq.(27)) and (Eq.(29)). **Figure 7** shows responses of the input signals (x_1, x_2, x_3) to the neural network and the output signal of workload y, represent the number of control events in a unit time. The dotted red color line indicates the output of trained neural network as estimated output, which reasonably matches with measured data of workload. **Figure 8** shows the estimated model parameter using the NPD method concerning the different data points. The variation of these parameters for the number of iterations is shown in **Figure 9**. As the number of iterations increases, the parameters attain a stable value of its estimates.

Unlike the OEM approach, initial values of model parameters are not needed in the application of NPD method, but it requires apriori structure of the model. The initial values of parameters are chosen as $\beta_1(0) = 0.0001, \beta_2(0) = 0.0001, \beta_3(0) = 0.0001$ for the application of output error method (OEM) in comparison. The responses of measured data of workload concerning control events and its estimated responses using OEM are given in **Figure 10**. and found that they are in close agreement with others. The results of the estimated parameters are tabulated in **Table 2**. The relative standard deviation of estimated parameters is computed in percentage and separately given in parenthesis. These values denote the confidence level of the corresponding estimate. It can be observed from **Table 2** that Neural Partial Differentiation (NPD) approach estimated parameters with less relative standard deviation compared to the output error method (OEM). As a result, estimated parameters of ATC dynamic model using NPD are more accurate in comparison with the Maximum likelihood (OEM) estimates.

The estimated ATC model is verified by the model validation as it is the last process in the model building procedure. For this, the complementary data set of input and output (other than the data used for the training of neural network) are used to predict the neural model of ATC. **Figure 11** shows how the measured response of workload compared with a predicted neural model of ATC and the estimated model by OEM. The validation of the model showed that match between the complement data response and predicted neural model response is good

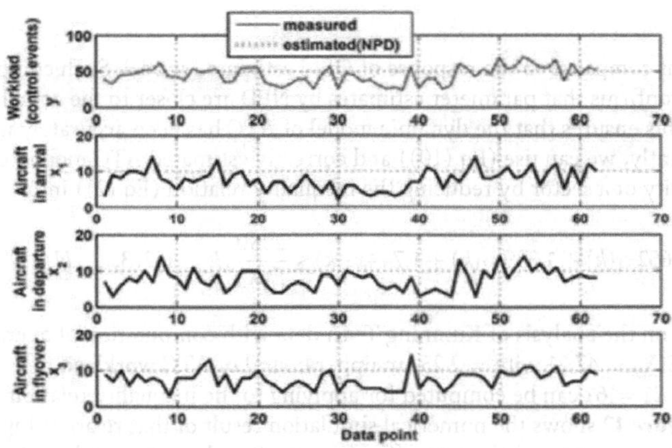

Figure 7.
Responses of measured data and neural dynamical model of ATC.

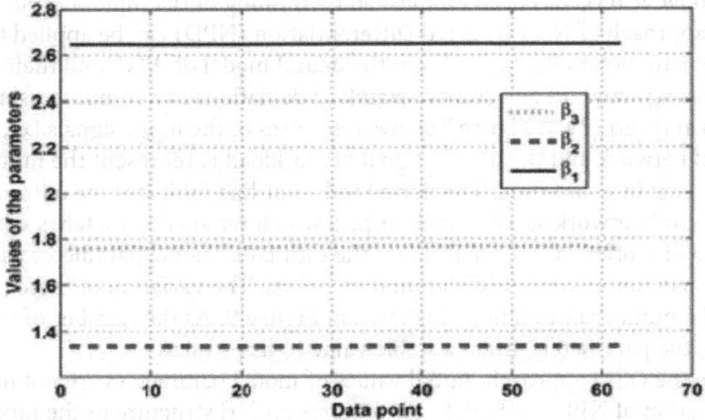

Figure 8.
Variation in estimated parameters with respect to data points using NPD.

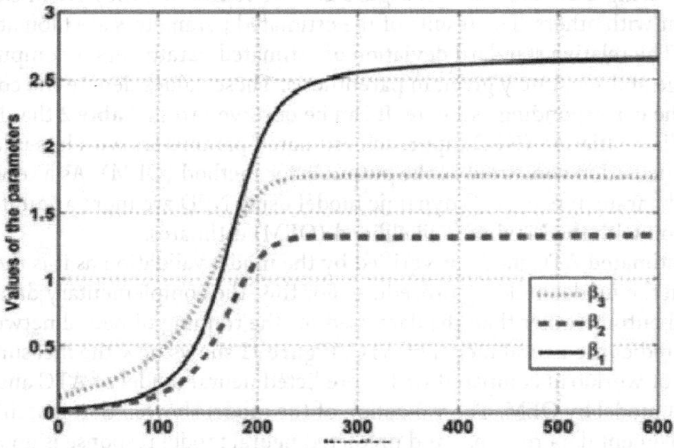

Figure 9.
Variation in estimated parameters w.r.t. number of iterations using NPD.

agreement compared to the response of OEM estimated model. Such compared result reconfirms that parameter estimates by NPD are closer to the actual values. Finally, this ensures that the dynamic model of ATC has been accurately identified. Subsequently, we can use (Eq.(10)) and correctly estimated ATC model to predict the capacity of a sector by reducing the inequality relation (Eq.(2)) into.

$$2.652x_1(k) + 1.339x_2(k) + 1.744x_3(k) \le \frac{2880}{E(X)}, k = 1, 2, 3, \dots, N \quad (31)$$

Based on the analysis of Kunming TMA data with computation of average time interval $E(X) = 47.21$ with = 2.25, an upper bound of ATC workload of (2880/47.21 =)61 can be computed for applying to the inequality relation (Eq. (31)). **Figure 12** shows the numerical simulation result of that relationship as a capacity curve to predict the air traffic capacity. Based on the number of flyover aircraft x_3, either possible cases of the number of arriving aircraft x_1 or the number of departing aircraft x_2 can be adjusted according to within the capacity curve. As a

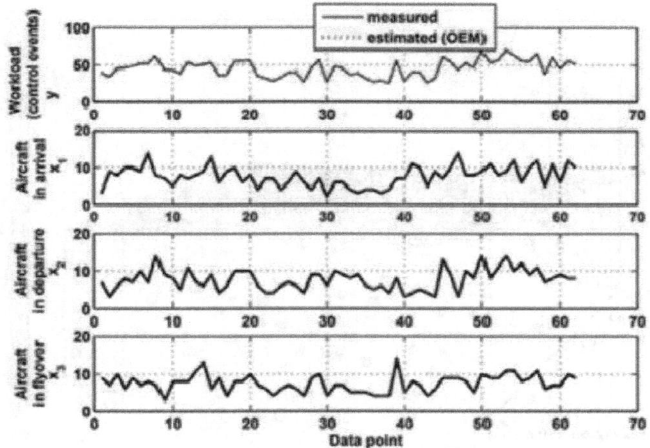

Figure 10.
Responses of measured and estimated workload using OEM.

Parameters	NPD	OEM
β_1	2.652 (2.52 [1])	2.8939 (2.90)
β_2	1.339 (2.405)	1.4634 (5.87)
β_3	1.744 (1.659)	1.5799 (7.16)

[1]*The values in parenthesis denote relative standard deviation values in percentage.*

Table 2.
Analysis of estimated parameters.

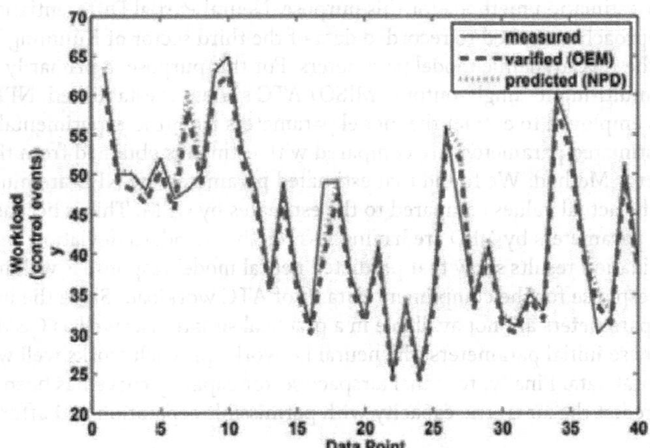

Figure 11.
Validation of estimated dynamic model of ATC.

result, air traffic capacity can be directly predicted from three-dimensional **Figure 12.** For a wide range of operation varies from less to more traffic congestion scenario with multi-dimensional tasks, postulated linear model might not be

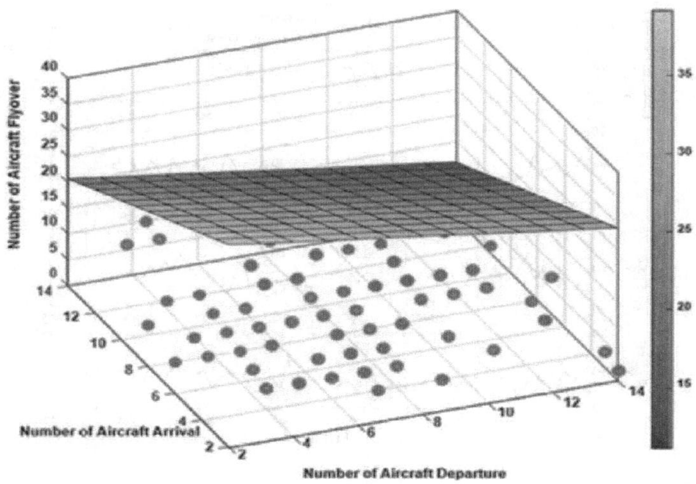

Figure 12.
Capacity curve.

sufficient to obtain a valid model of ATC. In such a case, research work on a nonlinear model of ATC can be considered as future work.

4. Conclusions

ATC dynamical model-based airspace sector capacity has been estimated. The Neural Partial Differentiation (NPD) and Output Error Method (OEM) are used as parameter estimation methods for this purpose. Neural Partial Differentiation (NPD) approach is applied to recorded data of the third sector of Kunming TMA to estimate the ATC dynamic model parameters. For this purpose, a primarily neural model of multi-input- single-output (MISO) ATC system is established. NPD method is employed to extract the model parameters from the experimental data, and the estimated parameters are compared with estimates obtained from the Output Error Method. We found that estimated parameters by NPD are much closer to the actual values compared to the estimates by OEM. This is because of 1) estimated parameters by NPD are having less relative standard deviation and 2) model validation results show that predicted neural model response is well matched with the response for the compliment dataset of ATC workload. Since the initial values of parameters are not available in a practical situation as well as OEM requires these initial parameters, the neural network approach works well with the experimental data. Finally, terminal airspace sector capacity curve has been developed to predict the air traffic capacity with permissible separation and affordable workload.

Acknowledgements

The author is grateful to thank Dr. Su Rong, faculty at NTU, Singapore, for carrying out this research work at Air Traffic Management Research Institute in Singapore.

Nomenclature

x_1	Total number of departing aircraft during an unit time
x_2	Total number of arriving aircraft during an unit time
x_3	Total number of flyover aircraft during an unit time
$\theta = \beta_1, \beta_2, \beta_3$	ATC model parameters
$G(.)$	Number of control events
e	Random error due to model uncertainty
S_{TD}	Standard deviation of data points
μ	Average of data points
R_{STD}	Relative standard deviation of estimates

Abbreviations

NPD	Neural Partial Differentiation
ATC	Air Traffic Controller
MISO	Multi Input Single Output
OEM	Output Eroor Method
TMA	Terminal Maneuvering Area
MLE	Maximum Likelihood Estimates

Appendix A: Output error method

In the output error method (OEM), the unknown parameters are obtained by minimization the sum of weighted square differences between the measured outputs and model outputs. The estimation problem is non-linear because of unknown parameter appears in the aircraft equations of motion and they are integrated to compute the states. Outputs are computed from states, control input and parameters using the measurement equation. Iterative nonlinear optimization techniques are required to solve this nonlinear estimation problem [28–30].

The mathematical model aircraft is assumed to be describe following general linear dynamics system representation.

$$\begin{aligned} \dot{x}(t) &= Ax(t) + Bu(t), x(t_0) = x_0 \\ y(t) &= Cx(t) + Du(t) \\ z(t_k) &= y(t_k) + v(t_k), k = 1, 2, 3, \ldots N \end{aligned} \tag{32}$$

where x is the $(n_x + 1)$ state variables, u the $(n_u + 1)$ control input vector, y the $(n_z + 1)$ system output vector, and measurement vector z is sampled at N discrete points. The Matrices A, B, C and D contain the unknown system parameters and are given by

$$\begin{aligned} \Theta = [&(A_{ij}, i = 1\ to\ n_x; j = 1\ to\ n_x)^T\ (B_{ij}, i = 1\ to\ n_x; j = 1\ to\ n_x)^T \\ &(C_{ij}, i = 1\ to\ n_y; j = 1, n_x)^T (D_{ij}, i = 1\ to\ n_y; j = 1\ to\ n_u\ )]^T \end{aligned} \tag{33}$$

In oder to estimates the likelihood function to estimates the parameter of dynamic system represented in (Eq.(32)), the following assumption:

- The exogenous input sequence $[u(t_k), k = 1, 2, 3 \ldots N]$ is independent of the system output.

- The measurement errors $[v(t_k) = z(t_k) - y(t_k)]$ at different discrete points are statically independent, the assume to be distributed with zero means and covariance matrix R, that is, $E\left(v(t_k) = 0, E\left[v(t_k)v^T(t_l)\right] = R\delta_{kl}\right.$

- The system is corrupted by measurement noise only.

- Control input $u(t_k)$ are sufficiently and adequately (i.e. in magnitude and frequency) varied to excite directly or indirectly the various modes of the dynamics system being analyzed.

The maximum likelihood output error estimates of unknown parameters are obtained by minimizing the negative logarithm of the likelihood function. **Figure 13** shows a block schematic of the output error method (OEM). The cost function of this method is considered in (Eq.(34)).

$$J(\Theta) = \frac{1}{2}\sum_{k=1}^{N}[z(t_k) - y(t_k)]^T R^{-1}[z(t_k) - y(t_k)] + \frac{N}{2}\ln|R| \tag{34}$$

Where is covariances matrix of the residuals and estimates can obtain from the (Eq.(35)). When started from suitably specified initial valus, the estimates are iteratively updated using Gauss-Newton method.

$$R = \frac{1}{N}\sum_{k=1}^{N}[z(t_k) - y(t_k)]^T[z(t_k) - y(t_k)] \tag{35}$$

The algorithmic steps of OEM are given below.

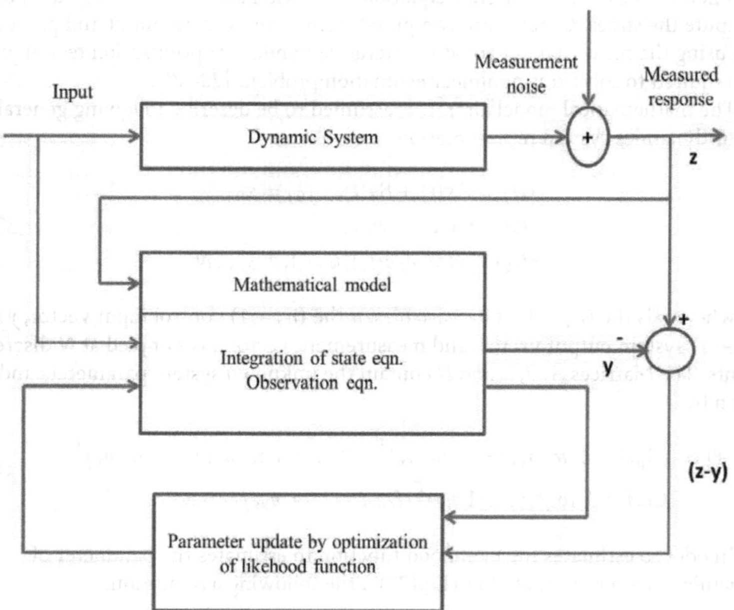

Figure 13.
Block schematic of the output error method.

Give the initial value of the Θ, i.e. Θ_0 . It may also consist of initial value of states x_0 if not known and biases in measurements Δz if required.

Step 1: Set iteration = 1.
Step 2: Compute the response and cost function J:

$$\begin{aligned}\dot{x}(t) &= Ax(t) + Bu(t)\\ y(t) &= Cx(t) + Du(t)\\ R &= \frac{1}{N}\sum_{k=1}^{N}[z(t_k) - y(t_k)]^T[z(t_k) - y(t_k)]\\ J &= \frac{1}{2}\sum_{k=1}^{N}[z(t_k) - y(t_k)]^T R^{-1}[z(t_k) - y(t_k)] + \frac{N}{2}\ln|R|\end{aligned} \tag{36}$$

Step 3: Perturb the parameter j, i.e., Θ_j to $\Theta_i + \Delta\Theta_i$, so that system matrices becomes $A_pB_pC_pD_p$.
Step 4: Compute the perturbation responses and update on Θ.

$$\begin{cases}\dot{x}_p(t) = A_p x_p(t) + B_p u(t)\\ y_p(t) = C_p x_p(t) + D_p u(t)\\ \dfrac{\partial y(t)}{\partial \Theta_j} = \dfrac{\left[y_p(t) - y(t)\right]}{\Delta \Theta_j}\\ \Delta_\Theta J(\Theta) = \sum_{k=1}^{N}\left[\dfrac{\partial y(t_k)}{\partial \Theta_j}\right]^T R^{-1}[z(t_k) - y(t_k)]\\ \Delta_\Theta^2 J(\Theta) = \sum_{k=1}^{N}\left[\dfrac{\partial y(t_k)}{\partial \Theta_j}\right]^T R^{-1}\left[\dfrac{\partial y(t_k)}{\partial \Theta_j}\right]\\ \Theta = \Theta + \left[\Delta_\Theta^2 J(\Theta)\right]^{-1}\left[\Delta_\Theta J(\Theta)\right]\end{cases} \tag{37}$$

Step 5: Increment the iteration count and jump back to step 2 to continue until the cost function reduces to zero approximately. Thus estimated parameter Θ is the updated at which cost function is minimized.

References

[1] Petersen, C., M. Mühleisen, and A. Timm-Giel. Modeling aeronautical data traffic demand. in Wireless Days (WD). 2016, March. IEEE.

[2] Habibullah, M. and M. Ahsanullah," Estimation of parameters of a Pareto distribution by generalized order statistics," Communications in Statistics-Theory and Methods. 29, no. 7 (2000): 1597–1609,

[3] Yifei, Z., et al." Method to analyze air traffic situation based on air traffic complexity map," Paper presented at 9th USA/Europe Air Traffic Management Research and Development Seminar (ATMf2011), Berlin, June, 2011.

[4] Basu, A., et al.," Geometric algorithms for optimal airspace design and air traffic controller workload balancing," Journal of Experimental Algorithmics (JEA). 14, (2010): 2–3,

[5] Irvine, D., et al.," A Monte-Carlo approach to estimating the effects of selected airport capacity options in London," Journal of Air Transport Management. 42, no.1–9 (2015),

[6] Leiden, K., P. Kopardekar, and S. Green." Controller workload analysis methodology to predict increases in airspace capacity," Paper presented at AIAA's 3rd Annual Aviation Technology, Integration, and Operations (ATIO) Forum, 2003.

[7] Hopkin, V.D., Human factors in air traffic control. (London: (Taylor & Francis, 1995).

[8] Majumdar, A." The crisis in European air traffic control: An assessment of controller workload modeling techniques," Paper presented at, 1996, Taylor & Francis Ltd.

[9] Majumdar, A. and W.Y. Ochieng, A Review of Airspace Capacity and Controller Workload Report to Eurocontrol. 2000: Contract No. C/1.108/H0/GC/99.

[10] Subotic, B., W. Ochieng, and A. Majumdar," Equipment failures in ATC: Finding an appropriate safety target," Aeronautical Journal. 109, (2005): 277–284, 10.1017/S0001924000000737.

[11] SIMMOD Simulation Airfield and Airspace Simulation Report, Oakland International Airport. 2006, ATAC Corporation.

[12] Hopkin, V.D., Human factors in air traffic control. (CRC Press, 2017).

[13] Hart, S.G.a.S., L.E., Development of the NASA-TLX (Task Load Index): Results of empirical and theoretical research, in Human Mental Workload. 1988: North-Holland.

[14] Wickens, C.D., et al., Engineering psychology and human performance.. 2015: Psychology Press.

[15] EUROCONTROL, AMS (Air Traffic Control Model Simulation Studies) - an introduction for potential users, in Internal EEC Note No. 2/AMS/1996, Model Based Simulations Sub-Division. 1996, EUROCONTROL: France.

[16] Magill, S.A.N. "Trajectory predictability and frequency of conflict-avoiding action," Paper presented at CEAS 10th International Aerospace Conference, Amsterdam, Netherlands, 1997.

[17] Welch, J.D., Andrews, J. W., Martin, B. D., and Sridhar, B., ." Macroscopic Workload Model for Estimating En Route Sector Capacity," Paper presented at Proceedings of the 7th ATM Seminar, Barcelona, Spain, July 2007.

[18] Majumdar, A., Ochieng, W. Y., McAuley, G., Lenzi, J. M., and Lepadatu,

C.," The Use of Panel Data Analysis Techniques in Airspace Capacity Estimation," Air Traffic Control Quarterly. 14, no.1 (2006): 95–115.

[19] Welch, J.D., Andrews, J. W., Martin, B. D., and Shank, E. M.,." Applications of a Macroscopic Model for En Route Sector Capacity," Paper presented at Proceedings of the AIAA Guidance, Navigation, and Control Conference, AIAA, Honolulu, Hawaii, August 2008.

[20] FAA. Order JO 7210.3 W facility operation and administration (2010), Report, U.S Department of Transportation.

[21] Mitchell, J.S.B., Polishchuk, V., and Krozel, J." Airspace Throughput Analysis Considering Stochastic Weather," Paper presented at Proceedings of the AIAA Guidance, Navigation, and Control Conference, Keystone, CO, August 2006.

[22] Krozel, J., Mitchell, J. S. B., Polishchuk, V., and Prete, J." Capacity Estimation for Airspaces with Convective Weather Constraints," Paper presented at Proceedings of the AIAA Guidance, Navigation, and Control Conference, ilton Head, SC, H, August 2007.

[23] Zou, J., Krozel, J. W., Krozel, J., and Mitchell, J. S. B." Two Methods for Computing Directional Capacity given Convective Weather Constraints," Paper presented at Proceedings of the AIAA Guidance, Navigation, and Control Conference, Chicago, IL, August 2009.

[24] Zhang, M., et al.," Terminal airspace sector capacity estimation method based on the ATC dynamical model," kybernetes. 45, (2016): 884–899, doi.org/10.1108/K-12-2014-0308.

[25] Bence Szamel., I.M., and Geza Szabo," Applying Airspace Capacity Estimation Models to the Airspace of Hungary," Periodica Polytechnica Transportation Engineering. 43, no.3 (2015): 120–128, doi.org/10.3311/PPtr.7512.

[26] Mohamed, M. and V. Dongare, Aircraft Aerodynamic Parameter Estimation from Flight Data Using Neural Partial Differentiation. 1st ed. Springer; 2021. DOI:10.1007/978-981-16-0104-0

[27] Laudeman, I.V., et al., Dynamic Density: An Air Traffic Management Metric. NASA-TM-1998-112226, April 1998.

[28] Maine, R. E. and Iliff, K. W. Identification of Dynamic Systems - Applications to Aircraft Part 1: The Output Error Approach AGARD, AG-300, 1986, 3.

[29] Majeed, M. and Kar, I. N. Identification of aerodynamic derivatives of a flexible aircraft using output error method Applied Mechanics and Material, Mechanical and Aerospace Engineering, 2012, 110–116, 5328–5335.

[30] Mehra, R.; Stepner, D. and Tyler, J. Maximum likelihood identification of aircraft stability and control derivatives Journal of aircraft, 1974, 11, 81–89.

Section 3

Human Factor

Chapter 6

Human Factors Quality Control in Air Traffic

Abstract

Every living person, from infants to older people, gets affected by internal and external factors. There are numerous researches and writings related to humans and these various factors. Human factors are recognized since the start of the human race. The awareness of the impacts of our environment is not new to humans. The focus in this chapter is upon those factors which can create an impact on aircraft mechanisms and air traffic controllers. These factors include human, psychological, work conditions, training, health conditions, environment, societal, and training. These factors must be quality controlled to minimize the errors in the critical domain of air traffic. A reduction in the number of errors will allow the performance to be higher and lowers the chances of fatal accidents.

Keywords: quality, human factors, qms, aviation

1. Introduction

Defining the term "Human Factors" is somehow challenging. When we think about the factors which may impact humans, it is understandable that the list is long and diverse from one person to another. It includes the diversified societal, geographical, and environmental differences related to those people. It possibly is more suitable to predict the concept instead of becoming entangled in setting an all-inclusive definition [1]. Any factor that impacts a human's performance anyhow then becomes of those beings that can be assessed to determine the impact upon the person. Trying to group these factors even into comprehensive groups can restrict our focus. Every person shares the majority of aspects to some extent. A reduced number of human factors may smear only to finite numbers of people or professions [2, 3].

Most of the factors which impact one group will influence the other with equivalent effect [4]. There are some features of the work for each group that makes them more inclined to affect by various factors and less so much from others. The communal thread, which relates these two groups, is concentration and focus. A deficiency can have calamitous consequences on the flying community [5, 6]. While air traffic controllers are at work at the moment of flight, it would make their requirement for focus and concentration more [7]. Still, when pondering the implication of a stick failure because of the lack of tightening a bolt or negligence of a moving part because of the lack of lubrication, it becomes evident that they were because of the lack of focus eventually the impact can have severe results. There are various kinds of work based on the common theme of aviation [8].

Moreover, the failure of a person to do efficiently has reflective impacts on protecting the National Air Space. Flight attendants have more awareness than the air traffic controllers than many aviation medical officers. However, some aviation medical officers perform physical tests on the air traffic controllers and understand the job responsibilities. As aviation officers do not have medical certifications, their importance and job function is not recognized by much of the aviation community, who do not directly contact them. A brief introduction to both kinds of work will be explained to understand the tasks of the environmental factors that may occur with either group [9]. Air Traffic Controllers can work commonly for five types of employers. Many of the civilian controllers are working under Federal Aviation Administration [10]. The other two nationally employed Air Traffic Controllers are those who are present on duty within the armed forces and those employed under Defense Department. Not all, but many smaller airfields had air traffic control services outsourced by the Federal Aviation Authority in some previous years. These Air Traffic Controllers are employed for private firms that manage the Federal Aviation Authority contract for that facility. Lastly are the private contract towers [11].

An example of this can be any airfield or Boeing field retaining air traffic controllers not assisting a federal contract. As the Federal Aviation Authority is involved with employee air traffic controllers, the remaining discussion will mainly be focused on this group. In this group, there are especially four sub-groups, sometimes stated as options. Three of them have direct responsibility and contact for guiding aircraft [12]. The fourth Autonomous Flight Safety System (AFSS) has a partial contract with aircraft in flight, based on the facility, first is the choice typically concepts of the public. Visual inspection is the pillar boosted by the usage of radar. As significant, complex fields radar is a virtual requirement [13]. They perform moving aircraft on the ground, aligning them for departure, and setting the preliminary headings instantly after departure [14]. They also have a responsibility for airplanes approaching the airport for landings. In three of the four options, the foremost task of the air traffic controllers is to help the pilot sustain the separation of their airplane from those around them [15]. The airport's size, the number of runways, and the schedule of departures and landings impact the work's complications; another option with a direct connection with the airplanes is the air route traffic control center (ARTCC). The kinds of facilities are for management of aircraft flying once they have recognized their air routes. They are not limited to commercial air transportation, though most of their traffic arrives from the higher altitude, lengthier distance type of flying. Radar is utilized for this control again. The facilities employ hundreds of controllers [16].

Automated Flight Service Stations (AFSS) are another type of air traffic control facility. They do not actively separate the aircraft; these stations get the flight schedules and provide weather details to the pilots for their flight route. They also help pilots in locating their position when they have no surety about their location. The usage of triangulation and radio does it [17, 18]. There are three types of work that fall under the aviation mechanic. The first one is the power plant mechanic. The second one is the airframe mechanic who performs the airframe and control services. As the name suggests, work performed has to do with the engine parts of the aircraft. The second type is the airframe mechanic, which works. Both power plants and airframe mechanics hold mechanical type certificates from the Federal Aviation Authority [19, 20].

A mechanic without a certificate may work on aircraft, though, requires to be under the direct regulation and control of another having a certificate. The third is the avionics personal integrated with the airplane's communication, radio, and compass elements. Again these elements contribute to a secure and safe .flight of the aircraft and vital tolls for the pilot [17]. Now we will look into the human quality factors of these occupations after refreshing the basics of the aviation mechanics and air traffic controllers. Instead of covering each vocation distinctly concerning each general element, it seems less monotonous to cover most aspects and explain how they impact the profession [21].

2. Health conditions

Air traffic controllers in the Federal Aviation Authority have health standards and go through regular check-ups based on the age and controllers' options. Except if employers cover them, mechanics do not possess a set of health standards [22]. The primary concern is those health conditions that can cause the person's abrupt and or subtle exhaustion. Definitely, during a crucial time in the control of an airplane, a sudden breakdown could be distressing. The area gets much of the concentration when recognizing the health clearance [23, 24]. Though just as challenging and correspondingly as troublesome are the subtle exhaustions, those conditions, though they do not take one off the job, similarly do not let employees perform at 100 percent of their potential. It would be the case of mild or moderate breathing issues, cardiac arrest untreated, the disturbing headache, and the whole extent of other conditions which are both disrupting and physically draining for any reason. Aside from climbing stairs to access a tower, most of the work is air traffic control is inactive or walking and standing in a comparatively small area [5, 25, 26].

Though the same cannot be assumed for the mechanic. They function in troublesome places and large working areas, as the physical issue can significantly impact their work [27]. Instead of grabbing the appropriate tool or seeing the manual, utilizing a shortcut or presumption in this area could prove distressing. Insufficient strength in fastening and unfastening the nuts and bolts because of the neurological or musculoskeletal condition could eventually generate a problem [28, 29]. Also, states that impact the entire agility could transform into a less than required work effort. These health conditions affect human factors, which ultimately create an impact on job performance. Because of the public trust and work's nature, these jobs differ from the typical professions [30, 31].

Keeping that recognition in mind is significant to avoid potentially adverse human factors [32]. Physical ability can have some impact on the job performance of both aviation mechanics and air traffic controllers. Height can act as an obstacle required to be handled by the air traffic controller [33]. The most common would be an individual height about the view from a tower or a piece of equipment. For the aviation mechanic, both height and body physique can generate issues. Because of the work's nature, sometimes convenience into a limited work area becomes a need of the job. If they cannot access the job, a different individual will perceptibly have to do that job [34]. The grave concern is when they have to work hard to body physique to perform the task. The work quality can be compromised, which would not be tolerable. When all probable, spaces to alleviate the impact of body physique should be raised [35]. Moreover, some people have physical traits which, for any reason, make their work much easier for them in comparison to their colleagues [36].

3. Psychological conditions

Distinct thinking and sustaining concentration and focus on tasks at hand are symbols of excellent performance in air traffic controllers and airplane mechanics.

Many professions need complete focus when working. It cannot be highlighted enough that these kinds of jobs, at times, do not endure errors [37, 38]. Numerous psychological conditions can impact workgroups, individual performance, and impact on other people's environments. Situational stress and depression states might be the most common mental conditions that can impact employees [39]. The extent of the effect on a person and his colleagues is pervasive and versatile. Then again, some people essentially explore comfort and relief in the workplace if situational stress is an outcome of factors outside of their employment [9, 40].

Many of them work without issues during those times as work allows a genuine break from specific problems and thoughts. These people seem to be those who entrenched the capability to concentrate while performing delicate parts of the safety of their job. It effectively becomes automatic when starting these jobs [22]. Others are not as self-controlled, allowing thoughts and feelings to interrupt and hinder their concentration and focus [41]. Indeed, if the work environment creates the root of the depression, then arriving at the workplace would not be a seamless situation [42, 43]. Those impacted by stress, colleagues, and managers require to keep in mind the changing character of the human mentality. It is always assumed that 90 percent of the issues are caused by ten percent of the employees [44]. The group of people who might not have adequately identified personality disorders, though their societal behaviors and character make them very problematic to manage in the workplace. Their colleagues and managers mainly recognize their impact. So these employees can easily make their problem, the problem of their workplace [43]. The condition can profoundly affect the workplace and creates a troublesome situation where such an individual is working. Then there are also employees with a direct personality disorder that either has been identified or identified if the individual ever required professional aid [6, 45].

Possibly the worst of ten percent, their vital task in life is to make enemies with people around them. The causes for these actions are recognized, and they generate disruption and devastation in the staff, which is very factual. Again because of the several regulations, rights, and rules all distinct employees get, it is problematic to handle them. Lastly, come those employees who may be honestly psychotic [46]. When they beat the clinical level, still have not performed obvious actions to cause their displacement, they are very troublesome [12, 47].

Many other conditions involving anxiety and depression leave the individual with the information that they are distressed and may not be appropriate for specific jobs. Not always so with the psychotic person [48]. There is no requirement for discussing the issues related to shifting the acts and thoughts of a delusional and paranoid individual to the radar screen, safe repairing of a powerplant, and skies. Workload, scheduling, budget, and various other factors make it very troublesome to recognize some of these problems. Identifying the potential issue would be the primary step which can be and is frequently impractical at times. However, the psychological factors which can generate an unfortunate outcome may well be close to the top of the list concerning the rate of occurrence [24, 49].

4. Societal issues

General society is just a reflection of several smaller social groups. There are people employed in and around the world of aviation from smaller groups, with fewer smaller groups confined within that world. Then there come the clicks which form in any work environment. As various flight specialists will recognize, an increased number of air traffic controller interviews, for any reason, make the declaration that they are the best in the system. The origin for this comes from a procedure in training future Air Traffic Controllers. It is perceived that they should have confidence and are told that they are the finest in the system. Now the reason here is deficient though the outcome of being inculcated in that way is fundamental. Not all air traffic controllers fall victim to that thought. However, many will repeat the phrase repeatedly as it is said that often saying something makes people feel that there can be any truth in the statement [50, 51]. The fundamental human factor issue comes from the lack of tolerance and competition that various air traffic controllers have. As they feel their plan is the only plan, it then follows that others must be doing it inaccurately. It can create unnecessary friction and discussion between the employees [52]. Moreover, if a person seriously thinks about it, there is a chance to obstruct the adapting or learning procedure. On the contrary, it could be said with rationality that competition is healthy. Societal characteristics, situations, and problems outside the workplace can influence anyone [22, 53].

5. Work conditions

As the total environment for a person can be segmented into various aspects, it is sometimes troublesome to keep these arbitrary divisions to the least. For example, working conditions will involve the physical setup of the workplace, equipment arrangement, accessibility of specific tools utilized in work performed [43, 54].

In the Air Traffic Controllers environment, the setting of equipment, towers, radios, displays, signal beacons, and other equipment segments can differ significantly from capacity to capacity. Research, study, time, and energy are invested in the settlement, arrangement of displays for computers and radar, display colors, chair types, and all the several equipment pieces required to perform their jobs [55]. Some management officials in the aviation industry feel there is an increased background noise during their connection with the flights. The noise comes from the air traffic controllers when they talk among themselves [56]. To avoid these, officials have placed carpeting in the trashcans to limit the sound of waste substances dropping to them [57, 58]. These are just utilized as instances of the thought procedures and considerations given to the alterations in the work environment of the air controllers. Another stimulating habit adopted by controllers, especially in the tower environment, is the rule recognized when approaching an air traffic controller on position the person wants to speak. Generally, the person will wait until the controller is talking on the radio before speaking to them. In the dynamic space, officials cannot understand if two persons speak at once but can talk to one and identify another person trying to speak to them [25, 26]. At a suitable time, the controller can identify the individual and start the conversation. The aviation mechanic is conditional to a more evolving environment based on the type of employer and work [59]. They can differ from working at the same place daily to working outside the airplane. The regulations and rules explain that they must have technical guides at hand when employed on an aircraft. The easy accessibility of these documents and manuals can influence their performance [10].

The settlements of the tools and equipment for them to carry out their tasks will make their jobs more accessible, and if they are not adequate for the job and cannot repair, it makes their work difficult [60]. The number of disruptions they may experience in their work and then the availability of the telephone will have an influence. When the mechanics are in the middle of servicing or assembling an airplane component, they require tracking the procedure and ensuring they finalize all the steps [61]. Not tightening a bolt or, in fact, over-tightening it can be destroyed. Working on some types of machinery can put the mechanic into a physical placement that can be uncomfortable and impact work performance [62].

6. Environment conditions

The temperature and lighting are appropriately controlled and kept persistent for the air traffic controller. The air traffic controllers work in the weather condition from a tower, and the mechanic may work in the weather. The tower controller has to handle the weather and night and day lightening at the different airports [59]. Again, it does not take much of an idea to visualize how the various times of day, cloud cover, and sun positioning can affect the tower cab [63]. At the same time, the temperature can vary slightly due to the comparatively large amount of glass present. The aviation mechanic does not have the same benefit when it comes to weather conditions at the controller. Functioning in extreme heat and cold can affect the health of a person [64].

7. Training

The inclusiveness and depth of training can differ from individual to individual and also between job types. There is an issue to permit access to training due to extensive contemplations and the demand on the other side when the academic procedure is completed. The all-inclusive and in-depth training is the better option. The air traffic controllers cannot understand if the training is too restricted even if the problem exists [36].

8. Conclusion

Various factors have been discussed in detail that allows the air traffic controllers, managers, quality management staff, quality control officers, auditors, employees, and people involved in the process improvement. However, the provided factors are a non-exhaustive list that could expand to other unknown or unknown factors. Everyone should play an important role in sustaining the high-quality levels and avoiding errors that could be fatal. Organizations need to measure their performance and monitor the error rate continuously to avoid any future accidents.

References

[1] Peißl, S., Wickens, C. D., & Baruah, R. (2018). Eye-tracking measures in aviation: A selective literature review. The International Journal of Aerospace Psychology, *28*(3-4), 98-112.

[2] Hopkin, V. D. (2017). *Human factors in air traffic control*. CRC Press.

[3] Yilmaz, A. K. (2019). Strategic approach to managing human factors risk in aircraft maintenance organization: risk mapping. Aircraft Engineering and Aerospace Technology.

[4] Pidgeon, N., & O'Leary, M. (2017). Organizational safety culture: Implications for aviation practice. In *Aviation psychology in practice* (pp. 21-43). Routledge.

[5] Lyu, T., Song, W., & Du, K. (2019). Human factors analysis of air traffic safety based on HFACS-BN model. Applied Sciences, *9*(23), 5049.

[6] Yang, Q., Tian, J., & Zhao, T. (2017). Safety is an emergent property: Illustrating functional resonance in Air Traffic Management with formal verification. Safety science, *93*, 162-177.

[7] Arinicheva, O., Dalinger, Y., Malishevskii, A., Sukhikh, N., & Khoroshavtsev, Y. (2018). Objectification of subjective estimation of abnormal cases danger in air traffic control. Transport Problems, *13*.

[8] Reva, O., Kamyshin, V., Borsuk, S., Shulgin, V., & Nevynitsyn, A. (2021, July). Qualitative Indexes of Air Traffic Controllers Attitude Toward Mistakes Hazard. In *International Conference on Applied Human Factors and Ergonomics* (pp. 618-624). Springer, Cham.

[9] Harle, P. G. (2017). Investigation of human factors: The link to accident prevention. In *Aviation psychology in practice* (pp. 127-148). Routledge.

[10] Manning, C., & Stein, E. (2017). Measuring air traffic controller performance in the 21st century. In *Human factors impacts in air traffic management* (pp. 303-336). Routledge.

[11] Chappell, S. L. (2017). Using voluntary incident reports for human factors evaluations. In *Aviation psychology in practice* (pp. 149-169). Routledge.

[12] Endsley, M. R. (2018). Expertise and situation awareness.

[13] Kistan, T., Gardi, A., & Sabatini, R. (2018). Machine learning and cognitive ergonomics in air traffic management: Recent developments and considerations for certification. Aerospace, *5*(4), 103.

[14] Alarcon, D. P. M., & Bieder, C. (2021, July). Producing Human Factor Recommendations in the Aviation Sector. In *International Conference on Applied Human Factors and Ergonomics* (pp. 228-236). Springer, Cham.

[15] Erjavac, A. J., Iammartino, R., & Fossaceca, J. M. (2018). Evaluation of preconditions affecting symptomatic human error in general aviation and air carrier aviation accidents. Reliability Engineering & System Safety, *178*, 156-163.

[16] Gatien, S., Gales, J., Khan, A., & Yerushalami, A. (2020, July). The importance of human factors when designing airport terminals integrating automated modes of transit. In *International Conference on Applied Human Factors and Ergonomics* (pp. 597-602). Springer, Cham.

[17] Yazgan, E. (2018). Development taxonomy of human risk factors for corporate sustainability in aviation sector. Aircraft Engineering and Aerospace Technology.

[18] Yıldırım, U., Başar, E., & Uğurlu, Ö. (2019). Assessment of collisions and grounding accidents with human factors analysis and classification system (HFACS) and statistical methods. Safety Science, *119*, 412-425.

[19] Kharoufah, H., Murray, J., Baxter, G., & Wild, G. (2018). A review of human factors causations in commercial air transport accidents and incidents: From to 2000-2016. Progress in Aerospace Sciences, *99*, 1-13.

[20] Shi, D., Zurada, J., & Guan, J. (2017, January). Identification of human factors in aviation incidents using a data stream approach. In *Proceedings of the 50th Hawaii International Conference on System Sciences*.

[21] Vascik, P. D., & Hansman, R. J. (2018). Scaling constraints for urban air mobility operations: air traffic control, ground infrastructure, and noise. In *2018 Aviation Technology, Integration, and Operations Conference* (p. 3849).

[22] Aricò, P., Borghini, G., Di Flumeri, G., Bonelli, S., Golfetti, A., Graziani, I., ... & Babiloni, F. (2017). Human factors and neurophysiological metrics in air traffic control: a critical review. IEEE reviews in biomedical engineering, *10*, 250-263.

[23] Bhardwaj, P., & Purdy, C. (2019, July). Safety and human factors for electronic flight bag usage in general aviation. In *2019 IEEE National Aerospace and Electronics Conference (NAECON)* (pp. 181-184). IEEE.

[24] Landman, A., Groen, E. L., Van Paassen, M. M., Bronkhorst, A. W., & Mulder, M. (2017). Dealing with unexpected events on the flight deck: a conceptual model of startle and surprise. Human factors, *59*(8), 1161-1172.

[25] Chen, Z., Guo, Z., Feng, G., Shi, L., & Zhang, J. (2021a, July). A qualitative study on the workload of high-speed railway dispatchers. In *International Conference on Human-Computer Interaction* (pp. 251-260). Springer, Cham.

[26] Chen, Z., Zhang, J., Jing, W., Peng, X., Ding, P., Chen, Y., ... & Zou, G. (2021b, July). A Preliminary Field Study of Air Traffic Controllers' Fatigue for Interface Design. In *International Conference on Human-Computer Interaction* (pp. 119-129). Springer, Cham.

[27] Triyanti, V., Azis, H. A., Prasetyawan, Y., & Iridiastadi, H. (2020, December). Individual Factors Related to Mental Workload in Air Traffic Controller. In *Joint Conference of the Asian Council on Ergonomics and Design and the Southeast Asian Network of Ergonomics Societies* (pp. 271-278). Springer, Cham.

[28] Güneş, Ç., & Töre Yargın, G. (2017). Affective human factors in aviation.

[29] Wan, M., Liang, Y., Yan, L., & Zhou, T. (2020). Bibliometric analysis of human factors in aviation accident using MKD. IET Image Processing.

[30] Patterson, E. S. (2018). Workarounds to intended use of health information technology: a narrative review of the human factors engineering literature. Human factors, *60*(3), 281-292.

[31] Taylor, J. C. (2017). *Risk management and error reduction in aviation maintenance*. Routledge.

[32] Wee, H. J., Lye, S. W., & Pinheiro, J. P. (2019, July). Monitoring Performance Measures for Radar Air Traffic Controllers Using Eye Tracking Techniques. In *International Conference on Applied Human Factors and Ergonomics* (pp. 727-738). Springer, Cham.

[33] Aguilar, J., Shi, D., Gutiérrez de Mesa, J. A., & Chávez, D. (2017). An Intelligent Model to Analyze Aviation Incidents.

[34] Song, H., Feng, K., & Zhang, Y. (2020, October). Study on Human Factor Evaluation of Aviation Maintenance During Flight Test. In *International Conference on Man-Machine-Environment System Engineering* (pp. 41-48). Springer, Singapore.

[35] Weiland, L. V., Law, C., & Sunjka, B. P. (2020). Ensuring sustainable and resilient air traffic management systems for South Africa with complexity and whole-of-society theory approaches. South African Journal of Industrial Engineering, *31*(3), 97-109.

[36] Muir, H. C., & Harris, D. (2017). *Contemporary issues in human factors and aviation safety*. Routledge.

[37] Kim, C. Y. (2019). A Study on Improvement of Aviation Maintenance Human Factors Training for Aviation Safety Promotion. Journal of the Korea Academia-Industrial cooperation Society, *20*(2), 115-121.

[38] Zimmermann, N., & Mendonca, F. A. C. (2021). The Impact of Human Factors and Maintenance Documentation on Aviation Safety: An Analysis of 15 Years of Accident Data Through the PEAR Framework. The Collegiate Aviation Review International, *39*(2).

[39] Maeng, S., & Itoh, M. (2021). Task Modeling in Air Traffic Control With Trajectorized en-Route Traffic Data Processing System. In *54th International Symposium on Aviation Psychology* (p. 244).

[40] Thoroman, B., Goode, N., Salmon, P., & Wooley, M. (2019). What went right? An analysis of the protective factors in aviation near misses. Ergonomics, *62*(2), 192-203.

[41] Edwards, T., Steely, R., Katz, A., & Lee, P. (2021). Behavioral Indicators in Air Traffic Control: Detecting and Preventing Performance Decline. In *39th International Symposium on Aviation Psychology* (p. 364).

[42] McDonald, N., Corrigan, S., Cromie, S., & Daly, C. (2017). An organisational approach to human factors. In *Aviation resource management* (pp. 51-61). Routledge.

[43] Orlady, H. W., Orlady, L. M., & Lauber, J. K. (2017). *Human factors in multi-crew flight operations*. Routledge.

[44] Xie, X., & Guo, D. (2018). Human factors risk assessment and management: process safety in engineering. Process Safety and Environmental Protection, *113*, 467-482.

[45] Arcúrio, M. S., Nakamura, E. S., & Armborst, T. (2018). Human factors and errors in security aviation: An ergonomic perspective. *Journal of Advanced Transportation, 2018*.

[46] Tarnavska, T., Baranovska, L., Glushanytsia, N., & Yahodzinskyi, S. (2021). The impact of psychological factor on the aircraft operation safety. In *E3S Web of Conferences* (Vol. 258, p. 02029). EDP Sciences.

[47] Lyall-Wilson, B., Kim, N., & Hohman, E. (2019, November). Modeling Human Factors Topics in Aviation Reports. In *Proceedings of the Human Factors and Ergonomics Society Annual Meeting* (Vol. 63, No. 1, pp. 126-130). Sage CA: Los Angeles, CA: SAGE Publications.

[48] Hrdinová, L., Hrdina, F., Krejsa, T., & Němec, V. (2019). Human Performance and its Impact on Aviation Safety. In *Transport Means: proceedings of the international scientific conference*. Kaunas University of Technology.

[49] Kontogiannis, T., & Malakis, S. (2017). *Cognitive engineering and safety organization in air traffic management*. CRC Press.

[50] Cardosi, K., & Lennertz, T. (2017). Human factors considerations for the integration of unmanned aerial vehicles in the national airspace system: An analysis of reports submitted to the aviation safety reporting system (ASRS).

[51] Mauriño, D. E. (2017). Proactive safety culture: Do we need human factors?. In *Aviation resource management* (pp. 1-9). Routledge.

[52] Pelegrin, C. (2017). The never-ending story of proceduralization in aviation. In *Trapping Safety into Rules* (pp. 13-25). CRC Press.

[53] Evans, A., Donohoe, L., Kilner, A., Lamoureux, T., Atkinson, T., Mackendrjck, H., & Kirwan, B. (2020). ATC, Automation and Human Factors: Research Challenges. In *Aviation Safety* (pp. 131-150). CRC Press.

[54] Zimmermann, K., Pariès, J., Amalberti, R., & Hummerdal, D. H. (2017). Is the aviation industry ready for resilience? Mapping human factors assumptions across the aviation sector. In *Resilience engineering in practice* (pp. 257-274). CRC Press.

[55] MacLeod, N. (2017). *Building safe systems in aviation: a CRM developer's handbook*. Routledge.

[56] Bongo, M., & Seva, R. (2021). Effect of Fatigue in Air Traffic Controllers' Workload, Situation Awareness, and Control Strategy. *The International Journal of Aerospace Psychology*, 1-24.

[57] Helmreich, R. L., & Merritt, A. C. (2017). *Culture at work in aviation and medicine: National, organizational and professional influences*. Routledge.

[58] Pittorie, W. P., Wilt, D. F., Rebensky, S., & Carroll, M. (2019). Low-Cost Simulator for Flight Crew Human-Factors Studies. In *AIAA Aviation 2019 Forum* (p. 2994).

[59] Fuller, R. (2017). Behaviour analysis and aviation safety. In *Aviation psychology in practice* (pp. 173-189). Routledge.

[60] Drogoul, F., & Cabon, P. (2021, July). Post COVID-19 Fatigue Management for ATCOs. In *International Conference on Applied Human Factors and Ergonomics* (pp. 319-323). Springer, Cham.

[61] Kluenker, C. S. (2021, July). Enhanced Controller Working Position for Integrating Spaceflight into Air Traffic Management. In *International Conference on Applied Human Factors and Ergonomics* (pp. 543-550). Springer, Cham.

[62] Stanton, N. A., Salmon, P. M., Walker, G. H., Baber, C., & Jenkins, D. P. (2017). *Human factors methods: a practical guide for engineering and design*. CRC Press.

[63] Li, Q., Ng, K. K., Fan, Z., Yuan, X., Liu, H., & Bu, L. (2021). A human-centred approach based on functional near-infrared spectroscopy for adaptive decision-making in the air traffic control environment: A case study. Advanced Engineering Informatics, 49, 101325.

[64] Patankar, M. S., & Taylor, J. C. (2017). *Applied human factors in aviation maintenance*. Taylor & Francis.

Chapter 7

Understanding Aviation English: Challenges and Opportunities in NLP Applications for Indian Languages

Abstract

English is a language that is understood, spoken and used by citizens of a diverse array of countries. The speakers include both native and non-native speakers of English. NLP or Natural Language Processing on the other hand is a branch of computer science that deals with one of the most challenging aspect that a machine can process: dealing with Natural Languages. Natural languages which have evolved over centuries are complete, diverse and highly complex and thus are challenging for a computer system to understand and process. MT or Machine Translation is a more specific part of NLP that translates one natural language to another (English being one of the major researched and sought after languages among them). Though research in the field of NLP and MT has come a long way and many efficient translators are available, still Translation and other NLP applications in specialized domains such as aeronautics are still today a challenge for NLP researchers and developers to achieve. NLP applications are often used in education of English Language, and are therefore a continuous process for Non-Native speakers of English. Non-native English speakers take help of various NLP tools such as E-Dictionary, MT applications and others to better understand the English language and thus learn it better and faster. Aviation English poses a challenge to MT systems and understanding it as a whole requires specialized handling as it has own phonetic pronunciations and terminologies and constituent Out-Of-Vocabulary words. Dealing with Aviation English calls for teaming up of experts from Applied Linguistics, NLP and AI. As a result it becomes a cross-research discipline that covers situations that demand real time use of proper language, e.g. ATC communications. This Paper aims to discuss most recent research methodologies that deals with the Aviation English and reviews the problems posed by it. Being a specialized and structured form of English, the problems are faced by both native and non-native speakers of English Language. Discussion is carried out in the relevant and recent advances of methods in dealing with aviation English language challenges from both, the Human (ICAO/DGCA/AAI) as well as NLP angle. Lastly we have a look at how these challenges are linked to scope for development of applied technologies. Research in experiential Aviation English situations deals with both English for Specific Purposes - ESP (Aeronautics in our case) as well as situations in English as a Foreign Language i.e. EFL (English-Indian language pair).

Keywords: English, Aeronautics, NLP, AAI, ICAO, DGCA

1. Introduction

In order to deal with specialized domains such as Aviation, Aero-Science, Aeronautics manufacturing and maintenance, Translation applications till today depends on Human assisted machine translation systems rather than fully automated and autonomous ones. The real challenge is posed by the unique structured words, OOV words and phraseologies that these domains consist of. One such domain is Aviation. It has evolved completely based on technical OOV words and sentences and has constantly enriched itself with words that are used in lieu of general English-Language words. For each and every component in aviation is unique and thus, this domain has evolved as a specialized branch making use of many but not all English-Language words. These words constitute the sentences in aviation and are thus untranslatable through standard translators like Google-Translate and Microsoft Translator Bing. In this paper, discussions will aim to provide a detail look at the constituent parts of the Aviation language and how it is a challenge for NLP applications such as Machine Translation. The discussion details how the Airport Authority of India and Director General of Civil Aviation (DGCA), India deals with training, testing and certification for Aviation English Language proficiency. The paper also has a look at how this domain has remained unexplored for Indian languages till the recent past. In the next phase the paper goes through the work that has been carried out for English-Bengali/other language pair. India being a country of non-native speakers of English Language makes it a challenging task. The scope that arises out of these challenges for researchers and developers are also discussed in the last section. Apart from databases and data repositories there happens to be a need for a well-researched and authored collection of tools and applications in English (monolingual) and English-other language pair (bilingual) that addresses the need for understanding and dealing with aviation English.

2. "ABC" of aviation English

Aviation domain demands that both the native and non-native speakers of English speak and spell the aviation words and sentences in the same way. This has been made possible by ICAO/DGCA which has fixed a standard dialog that is to be followed by all aviators, ATC controllers, ground crew, and maintenance and operation staff among others. Aircrafts and airlines are identified by their country of origin (VT for India) by combination of English alphabets (Alpha-Bravo-Charlie for ABC). The phonetic pronunciations of these alphabets are also fixed by the ICAO. **Table 1** shows how the phonetic pronunciation of numbers in aviation, while **Table 2** show the English alphabets equivalent.

ICAO prescribed phonetic pronunciation for Numbers	0: ZE-RO	7: SEV-en
	1: WAN	8: AIT
	2: TOO	9: NIN-er
	3: TREE	Decimal: DAY-SEE-MAL
	4: FOW-er	Hundred: HUN-dred
	5: FIFE	Thousand: TOU-SAND
	6: SIX	—

Table 1.
Phonetics for roman numbers as prescribed by ICAO [1, 2].

A: AI-FAH (ALFA)	B: BRAH-VOH (BRAVO)	C: CHAR-LEE (CHARLIE)
D: DELLTAH(DELTA)	E: ECK-OH(ECHO)	F: FOKS-TROT (FOXTROT)
G: GOLF (GOLF)	H: HOH-TEL (HOTEL)	I: IN-DEE-AH (INDIA)
J: JEW-LEE-ETT (JULIET)	K: KEY-LOH (KILO)	L: LEE-MAH (LIMA)
M: MIKE (MIKE)	N: NO-VEM-BER (NOVEMBER)	O: OSS-CAR (OSCAR)
P: PAH-PAH (PAPA)	Q: KEH-BECK (QUEBEC)	R: ROW-ME-OH (ROMEO)
S: SEE-AIR-RAH (SIERRA)	T: TANG-GO (TANGO)	U: YOU-NEE-FORM (UNIFORM)
V: VIK-TAH (VICTOR)	W: WISS-KEY (WISKEY)	X: ECKS-RAY (XRAY)
Y: YANG-KEY (YANKEE)	Z: ZOO-LOO (ZULU)	—

Table 2.
Phonetics for alphabets as prescribed by ICAO [1, 2].

Going by the above example if a flight is registered as "VT-SCA", where "VT" means "VICEROYs TERRORITY" that is, the aircraft is registered with DGCA (INDIA). If it is to be addressed by the ATC as then controller will pronounce it as "VICTOR TANGO -SIERRA CHARLIE ALFA". The same pattern is followed for all documentation such as incident reports, maintenance manuals and paper works in the aviation domain.

3. Aviation "Out of Vocabulary" words and phraseologies

Aviation sentences consist of structured and standard OOV words and phraseologies combined with normal English words. Common example of such technical sentences is Notice to Airmen, better known as "NOTAM". Aviation makes use of unique unheard of OOV words that are unique only to it. Example includes terms such as aircraft are known as ACFT, FL for Flight Level and such.

Name of airport	IATA code	ICAO code
Bagdogra	IXB	VEBD
Heathrow	LHR	EGLL
Los Angeles	LAX	KLAX
Patna	PAT	VEPT
Agartala	IXA	VEAT

Table 3.
IATA and ICAO codes for a few airport names.

Aviation OOV	Meaning in English
Circuit	To circle at a particular altitude
Front Gear	Set of wheels at the front
ALT	Altitude
FLT	Flight
EBOUND	Going towards East

Table 4.
Aviation OOV words and their meanings in English.

All documentations in aviation, airports are known by either IATA location identifier or by ICAO four letter arrangements which are unique only to that particular airport. These arrangements are used by people related to aviation irrespective of them being Native or Non-Native speakers of English. The IATA and ICAO code of a few airports are as depicted in **Table 3**. We can see in **Table 3**, while IATA codes are all 3 letter words, ICAO are 4 letters. IATA stands for International Air Transport Association, while ICAO means International Civil Aviation Organization. Arrangements as such make hundreds of OOV words and have formed the basic vocabulary for aviation related documents. **Table 4** presents with some examples of OOV words used in aviation.

4. Exploring the language aspect of AAI manual of air traffic services

India being a country of non-native speakers of the English language, Airport authority of India has made available-online the Manual of Air Traffic Services [3] for references of concerned parties. There are 17 chapters that can are listed in **Table 5**. In the table it can be observed that out of the 17 Chapters, Chapter 12 is concerned with the aviation phraseologies. Chapter 12 highlights how the OOV aviation words and general English sentences are combined together to form the various unique terminologies that are accepted all throughout the aviation domain. Chapter 14 emphasizes on the ATC-Pilot communications, which is again in aviation English. Chapter 15 highlights the procedures for communication over the communication channel. To get a better idea of phraseologies used in aviation let us take a look at some examples and their respective meanings (**Table 6**).

Chapter number and name	Chapter number and name	Chapter number and name	Chapter number and name	Chapter number and name	Chapter number and name
1. Document Identification and control	2. Definitions	3. General	4. Air Traffic Services (ATS)	5. Separation Methods and Minima	6. Procedures in the vicinity of aerodromes
7. Aerodrome control Services	8. Radar Services and Procedures	9. Flight information Services	10. Coordination	11. ATS Messages	12. Phraseologies
13. ADS services	14. Controller-Pilot data link communications	15. procedures for communication failures, etc	16. Miscellaneous Procedures	17. ATS Safety Management	

Table 5.
AAI MATS layout.

Aviation Phraseologies / Phrases	Meaning
RVR NOT AVAILABLE	Runway Visible Range not available
CANCEL OFFSET	Instruction to rejoin cleared flight route or other information
MAINTAIN VMC	Maintain visual meteorological conditions

Table 6.
Example of AAI MATS CHAPTER 12 phraseologies.

There are hundreds of aviation phraseologies spanning from aircraft identification to holding pattern that has to be known to people working in the aviation sector, especially pilots and ATC controllers. These phraseologies are arrangements of specific aviation domain words and general English ones.

5. DGCA aviation English language proficiency training, test and certification

DGCA, India has devised a complete systematic procedure that provides training in real time application of Aviation English Language. It also covers radio-telephony English knowledge acquisition and communication skills over RF involving simulated and real time learning environments for English as a Foreign specialized language. As a case study the authors discusses in detail the way AEL is trained, tested and certified for the cadets/ candidates. The main aim of DGCA is to make sure that an applicant for Pilot license, ATC personnel, aircraft engineer and route navigator license to have the capability to communicate and understand the aviation English language used through RT to the level of required proficiency [4]. The CAR or better known as Civil Aviation Requirement is available according to the provisions of Aircraft rules of 1937-133A. It lays down the procedures for Training, Testing and Certification for Aviation English Language proficiency. The following **Table 7** gives us an idea of the candidates, evaluators, measures, metrics and measurements used to evaluate the Aviation English Language proficiency.

The multiple stages for proficiency in English language are as depicted in **Table 8**. The assessment parameters have 6 areas of specialization which are:

Applicable to	Evaluator	Measures	Measurements	Metrics
A holder of Pilot's (PP License, CP License, Airline Transport Pilot's License (Fixed and rotary wings) A holder of Flight Engineer's License Route Navigator's License An holder of Air Traffic Services Personnel License	Interlocutor	Language proficiency skills	Descriptor	*Minimum Age:* 16 years
	Operational rater or Operational assessor		Rating scale	*Educational qualification*: Class 10 or equivalent
	Rater or Assessor			*Training:* 200 to 400 hours of aviation English language training

Table 7.
DGCA aviation English language proficiency testing layout.

Stage	Meaning	Acceptable?	Re-evaluate?-further action
1	Pre-elementary	No	More training suggested
2	Elementary	No	More training suggested
3	Pre-operational	No	More training suggested
4	Operational	Yes	Yes, after 6 years
5	Extended	Yes	Yes, after 6 years
6	Expert	Yes	No Re-evaluation required

Table 8.
DGCA aviation English proficiency stages.

pronunciation, structure, vocabulary, fluency, comprehension and interactions. Together they determine the linguistic performance of the candidate.

6. Language loss and deterioration

It is commonly observed from experience and practical observation that for non-native speakers of English, language loss is quite common. Deterioration in language proficiency of candidates for whom English is not the 1st language is also a common trait. In cases as such, candidates' proper re-evaluation and assessment may be conducted according to ICAO norms for Aviation English. DGCA and other aviation regulatory bodies around the world endorse such progress.

7. The NLP angle

Natural Language Processing or in short NLP is an interesting branch of research that encompasses Artificial Intelligence, Neural Networks, Linguistics and an array of Natural Languages such as English, French etc. It aims to provide seamless translation from one natural language to another through translation and transliteration, among other applications such as part-of-speech tagging and E-dictionary. Though the use of monolingual NLP applications is found in the modern aviation services (IBM WATSON [5], AMRIT [6], BLEU [7] and PLUS [8]), it is hard and almost impossible to find bilingual translation services in regular real time use. The same goes for all Indian languages. Apart from incorporating the underlying rules of the concerned natural languages NLP has always strived to create monolingual and bilingual corpora that can assist in the translation and transliteration of the various natural languages. Specialized English applications such as Aviation / Aeronautics and similar streams have always posed a challenge to achieving the goals of NLP applications. The use of structured English words in aviation not only prevents proper translation but also Transliteration. Let us look at some examples of the mentioned problems.

8. Problem with direct translation and transliteration

The aviation OOV words cannot be directly translated and transliterated by standard translation applications like Google Translate and Microsoft translator

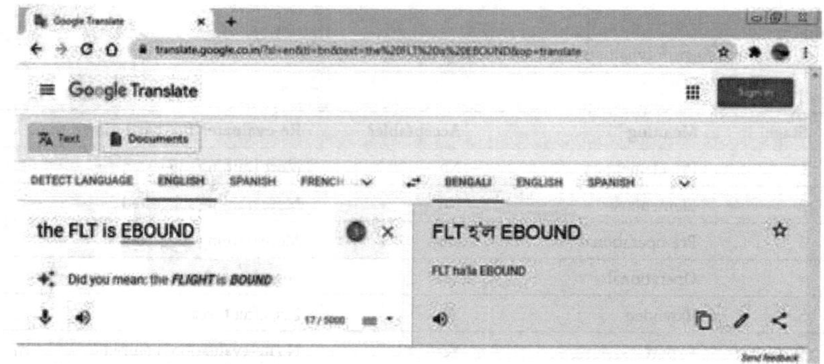

Figure 1.
Inability of Google TRANSLATE in handling aviation OOV words.

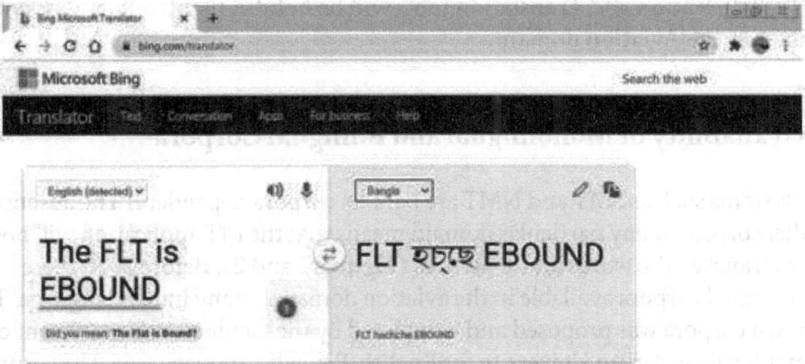

Figure 2.
Inability of Microsoft BING in handling aviation OOV words.

Bing. Multiple attempts to translate and transliterate them have resulted in failure. **Figures 1** and **2** shows the inability of standard translators to transliterate aviation OOV word.

9. Unavailability of E-dictionary and standard translation work

While standard E-Dictionaries are available in both online and offline form and in soft and hard copies it is special domains such as aviation where E-Dictionaries are not available. Before 2017 apart from TUAM-AVIATION [9] no translation/transliteration work was taken up for aviation maintenance manuals, navigation manuals or such. This makes the work of dealing with aviation sequences all the more challenging.

10. Complex situation with Indian languages

Though in European countries and the USA (ASRS) [https://asrs.arc.nasa.gov/] some attempts has been made to document maintenance, guidance and incident reports and manuals in the soft format and online versions, In India, no such attempts has been made. Although DGCA [http://dgca.nic.in/] maintains incident and accident summaries involving those happening in Indian Airspace, these reports are saved in PDF format. No attempt has been made to store these reports in a centralized repository, that can be used for further research or mining. These reports are neither categorized nor segmented, thus making them unsuitable for research and development purposes. Though TDIL (https://tdil.meity.gov.in/) holds a wide variety of Indian corpora and tools still resources for aeronautics and aero-space domain are completely absent. Making the matter more complex no database or corpora in India along with options for corresponding pronunciation, phonetic representation and meaning in any Indian languages are available for the aviation domain. Transliteration and Translation applications for Indian languages in aviation and aeronautics domain are non-existent. Though English is the medium of instruction in many institutions in India for non-native speakers of English, the availability of corresponding terms of these abbreviations in Indian languages and their meaning are a different aspect altogether. For many who wish to make into the lucrative career of maintenance, ATC, support staff and aviation-related jobs these transliteration and translation will be of much help. With the huge number of MRO and aircraft manufacturing companies starting production factories in

India, Transliteration and Translation tools will be helpful in introducing potential candidates to the Aviation domain.

11. Unavailability of Monolingual and Bilingual Corpora

MT systems such as SMT and NMT are parallel corpora dependent. The absence of parallel corpus for any particular domain means that the MT application will not be able to translate the words and sentences (**Figures 1** and **2**). Before 2020 there were no parallel corpora available in the aviation domain for any Indian language. The first known corpora was proposed and completed by the faculties of Department of Computer Science, Assam University for English-Bengali Language pair. The corpus was developed, keeping in mind the complexity of the aviation domain and the vocabulary size was determined through OpenNMT while training the NMT system. Given its uniqueness, the corpus consists of hundreds of aviation OOV words and phraseologies. The Corpus was made to go through pre-processing steps and thus cleaned, tokenized and lemmatized (for both English and Bengali languages). The source of the English aviation sentences ranges from NASA ASRS reports to AAI and DGCA reports.

12. Scope in MT and NLP

The challenges posed by aviation domain in the field of NLP, especially for Machine Translation also create a huge scope for researchers and developers. It is an unexplored avenue that needs immediate attention. It can open up huge opportunity for researchers in the form of creating monolingual and bilingual corpora, both Preprocessing and post-processing tools and E-dictionaries among others. Some important work that has been carried out by faculties of Computer Science, Assam University, Silchar for the English-Bengali language pair in the aviation domain are as listed in the following **Table 9** [1, 2, 10, 11].

Thus scope of work exists in implementation of E-Dictionary, Pre-processing tools, Post-Processing tools, text analyzers, and MT systems between English and Indian native languages for aviation, aero-space and other specialized and technical domains.

Name of the paper	Contributions	Published in
NLP tools used in civil aviation, A survey. (S. Paul B.S. Purkyastha, P. Das)	Survey and Identification of NLP tools used in the aviation Domain	IJARCS, Vol 9., No.2, March –April 2018, ISSN: 0976–5697, Page:110–114
English to Bengali Transliteration tool for OOV words common in Indian civil aviation (S. Paul, B.S. Purkaystha)	Design and Development of 1st known transliteration tool of aviation OOV words for English-Bengali language pair	JADMS, Volume 6, issue 1, April 2019, ISSN: 2393–8730
Bilingual Technical E-Dictionary for aviation OOV words. (S. Paul, B.S. Purkhyastha)	Design and Development of 1st known E-Dictionary for Aviation OOV words for English-Bengali pair	IJEAT,Volume9, issue 2, December 2019, ISSN:2249–8958
Handling Aviation OOV words for Machine translation and corpus creation	Design and Development of Corpus Creation tool. Translation Assistance tool for Bengali language	IJCSE, Volume 11, No.5 Sep-Oct-2020, ISSN: 0976–5166

Table 9.
List of work in the field of aviation domain for English-Bengali language pair.

13. Importance of achieving phonetic equivalence

Aviation/Aeronautics English consists of OOVs, Phrases and Phraseologies in their hundreds, as a result in order to create a parallel corpus for English-Indian language requires us not only to create the native language equivalent translation but also the phonetic equivalent terms of the aviation OOV words. Phonetic equivalence of OOV words can be created through use of a standard phonetic keyboard for that particular language. For Bengali the AVRO keyboard is a handy tool. **Figure 3** depicts the phonetic layout for the Avro Keyboard. Phonetic equivalent words are useful for development of transliterated words. Transliterated words play a huge role in creation of aviation and technical corpora / database.

14. Conclusion and future scope

The native Indian languages present a huge scope for researchers to work on, specially for technical and unexplored domains. Though untouched till 2017, but work has begun on the aviation domain for Indian languages (English-Bengali pair) and we can conclude with the following points: The first known implementation of English-Indian language NMT based MT system for the aviation domain has been carried out and published with satisfactory results, is documented as "Detailed analysis of successful implementation of aviation NMT system and the effects of aviation post-processing tools on TDIL tourism corpus", Saptarshi Paul, Bipul Syam Purkaystha, Journal of KING SAUD university-computer and information sciences [12].

Scope exists for development of English-other native Indian languages MT systems and NLP tools.

Development of MT systems for specialized and technical domains such as Aero-Space, Aircraft Maintenance manuals etc. are still unexplored.

Future Scope of research and work exists for NLP applications for Foreign Languages- Indian Languages pair as well as Indian- Indian Languages pair too. We can list some of them as follows:

Creation of Chat bots for the aviation domain in Indian languages: This application can help in reaching out to target audience and potential customers, chat bots are already in use for various tourism sites and can be easily extended for aviation related applications and WebPages.

Development of E-dictionary for Indian languages: As Indians are all non-native speakers of English so huge scope prevail in creation of aviation / aero-science E-Dictionaries.

Development of aviation Machine Translation systems: This application can find its use with travelers as well as people related with aviation industry. The

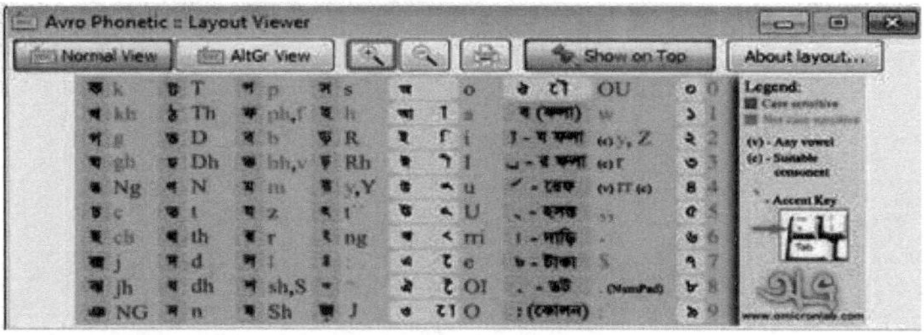

Figure 3.
Avro keyboard layout.

ability to translate aviation related sentences from English/French to an array of Indian languages can also help people engaged in aviation sector in faster and better understanding the maintenance manuals of Boeing/Airbus/ATR etc. The above mentioned applications can all find its way into maintenance, repair, operations, and aeronautics training institutes. Apart from the mentioned points, academic interests may include development of Email filters, Smart assistants, Predictive analysis Digital phone calls, Data analysis and Text analytics among others for aviation sentences.

Though only a handful of NLP tools have been developed for English and Indian languages, the number of Translation tool is restricted to only one [13], that too at an experimental level.

Translation Tools between English and Indian Languages can not only be helpful for travelers but also for aspiring candidates appearing for various airlines regulatory bodies such as DGCA and AAI.

The non-native speakers of English can greatly benefit from these tools and MT applications in enhancing their skills and thus improving their chances of clearing the various tests and ultimately fulfilling their dream of reaching out to the sky.

References

[1] Saptarshi paul, Bipul shyam purkhyastha, "NLP tools used in civil aviation: A Survey", International journal of advanced research in computer science, volume 9, Number 2, March-April-2018

[2] Saptarshi Paul, Bipul Shyam Purkhyasta. English to Bengali Transliteration Tool for OOV words common in Indian Civil Aviation. Journal of Advanced Database Management & Systems. 2019; 6(1): 23-32p.

[3] AAI MATS, (1995). Available from: https://www.aai.aero/en/system /files/ resources/1%20Commercial% 20Manual%202019.pdf [Accessed: 2020/11/27]

[4] DGCA reports, (1999). Available from: http://dgca.nic.in/accident/ reports /contents_acc_rep.html [Accessed: 2020/07/18]

[5] IBM WATSON, (2010), Available from: https: //www.ibm.com/watson/ stories /aviation.html [Accessed: 2017/10/10]

[6] NLP in AIRBUS (2016). Available from: http://www.intelligentaerospace. com / pt / 2016 / 10/21/applying-natural-learning-processing-to-airbus-helicopters.html [Accessed: 2021/02/27]

[7] NLP in MRO (2015). Available from: http://aviationweek.com/aviation-maintenance-and-support-software/ applying-natural-learning-processing-airbus-helicopters[Accessed: 2020/12/02]

[8] Peter Clark and Phil Harrison, "Boeing's NLP System and the Challenges of Semantic Representation" WA 98124, ACL, STEP '08 Proceedings of the 2008 Conference on Semantics in Text Processing, Pages 263-276, Venice, Italy, September 22 - 24, 2008 .

[9] Pierre Isabelle and Laurent Bourbeau, "TAUM-AVIATION: its Technical Features and some experimental Results", Computational Linguistics, Volume 11, Number 1, January-March 1985. Pages: 18-27.

[10] Saptarshi paul, Bipul Shyam Purkhyasta "Bilingual (English to Bengali) Technical E-Dictionary for Aviation OOV Words", International journal of Engineering and advanced technology, volume 9, issue 2, December 2019

[11] Saptarshi Paul, Bipul Shyam Purkhyasta. English to Bengali Transliteration Tool for OOV words common in Indian Civil Aviation. Journal of Advanced Database Management & Systems. 2019; 6(1): 23-32p.

[12] Saptarshi Paul, Bipul Syam Purkaystha, "Detailed analysis of successful implementation of aviation NMT system and the effects of aviation post-processing tools on TDIL tourism corpus", Journal of KING SAUD university-computer and information sciences, ISSN: 1319-1578, publisher: ELSEVIER https://doi.org/10.1016/j. jksuci.2021.01.016, 2021.

[13] Bipul Syam Purkaystha, Saptarshi Paul "English to Bengali Neural Machine Translation System for the Aviation Domain", Infocomp Journal of Computer Science E-ISSN: 1982-3363, Vol. 19, No. 2, December 2020, pp. 78-97

Index